The Twelve Conditions of a Miracle

TODD MICHAEL

JEREMY P. TARCHER / PENGUIN

A MEMBER OF PENGUIN GROUP (USA) INC.

NEW YORK

The
TWELVE
CONDITIONS
of a
MIRACLE

Dr Todd Michael

The Miracle Worker's Handbook

Celebration Church

JEREMY P. TARCHER/PENGUIN
Published by the Penguin Group
Penguin Group (USA) Inc., 375 Hudson Street, New York, New York 10014, USA • Penguin Group
(Canada), 90 Eglinton Avenue East, Suite 700, Toronto, Ontario M4P 2Y3, Canada (a division of
Pearson Canada Inc.) • Penguin Books Ltd, 80 Strand, London WC2R 0RL, England • Penguin Ireland,
25 St Stephen's Green, Dublin 2, Ireland (a division of Penguin Books Ltd) • Penguin Group
(Australia), 250 Camberwell Road, Camberwell, Victoria 3124, Australia (a division of Pearson Australia
Group Pty Ltd) • Penguin Books India Pvt Ltd, 11 Community Centre, Panchsheel Park,
New Delhi–110 017, India • Penguin Group (NZ), 67 Apollo Drive, Rosedale, North Shore 0632,
New Zealand (a division of Pearson New Zealand Ltd) • Penguin Books (South Africa) (Pty) Ltd,
24 Sturdee Avenue, Rosebank, Johannesburg 2196, South Africa

Penguin Books Ltd, Registered Offices: 80 Strand, London WC2R 0RL, England

First trade paperback edition 2008
First Jeremy P. Tarcher edition 2004
Originally published by Abundance Media, 2001.

Greek text adapted from *The Interlinear Bible*, second edition,
Jay P. Green, Sr., General Editor and Translator, Henrickson Publishers,
1986. Used with the permission of the copyright holder. Copyright 1976,
the Trinitarian Bible Society, London.

Most Tarcher/Penguin books are available at special quantity discounts for bulk
purchase for sales promotions, premiums, fund-raising, and educational needs.
Special books or book excerpts also can be created
to fit specific needs. For details, write Penguin Group (USA) Inc.
Special Markets, 375 Hudson Street, New York, NY 10014.

The Library of Congress catalogued the hardcover edition as follows:

Michael, R. Todd.
The twelve conditions of a miracle : the miracle worker's handbook / by R. Todd Michael.
p.   cm.
Rev. ed. of : The twelve conditions of a miracle / Michael Abrams. 2001.
ISBN 1-58542-352-1
1. Feeding of the five thousand (Miracle).   2. Miracles.   I. Abrams, Michael. Twelve
conditions of a miracle.   II. Title.
BT367.F4M53   2004   2004048012
226.7'06—dc22

ISBN 978-1-58542-673-7 (paperback edition)

Printed in the United States of America
1   3   5   7   9   10   8   6   4   2

Book design by Jennifer Ann Daddio

While the author has made every effort to provide accurate telephone numbers and Internet addresses
at the time of publication, neither the publisher nor the author assumes any responsibility for errors, or
for changes that occur after publication. Further, the publisher does not have any control over and does
not assume any responsibility for author or third-party websites or their content.

IN MEMORY OF CLAYTON B. PILCHER

You taught me everything I needed to know,

in your garden,

while yet a child.

AND FOR JULIAN

who teaches me now.

"AND EVEN GREATER

WORKS THAN THESE

YOU WILL DO"

— JOHN 14:12

CONTENTS

PREFACE

A brief explanation is in order to "decode" the text that precedes each chapter of the book. Here is a sample of this text for discussion purposes.

> εὐλόγησε
> e v l o g i s e
> **He blessed**

Throughout the book, the first line of these characters represents the original Greek for the passage found in Matthew 14:13–20. The second line is a transliteration of Greek into Roman characters. Finally, the third line represents the orthodox translation of each word.

The entire passage follows in this format.

Καὶ ἀκούσας ὁ Ἰησοῦς ἀνεχώρησεν ἐκεῖθεν ἐν
Kai akousas o Iisous anechorisen ekeithen en
And hearing Jesus withdrew from there in

πλοίῳ εἰς ἔρημον τόπον κατ᾽ ἰδίαν καὶ ἀκούσαντες
ploio eis eremon topon kat idian kai akousantes
a boat into a desert place privately and having heard

οἱ ὄχλοι ἠκολούθησαν αὐτῷ πεζῇ ἀπὸ τῶν πόλεων.
oi ochloi ikolouthisan auto pezi apo ton poleon.
the crowd followed Him on foot from the cities.

Καὶ ἐξελθὼν ὁ Ἰησοῦς εἶδε πολὺν ὄχλον,
Kai exelthon o Iisous eide polun ochlon,
And going out Jesus saw great a crowd,

καὶ ἐσπλαγχνίσθη ἐπ᾽ αὐτούς, καὶ
kai esplanchyisthi ep autous, kai
and was filled with pity toward them, and

ἐθεράπευσε τοὺς ἀρρώστους αὐτῶν.
etherapefse tous arrostous auton.
He healed the infirm of them.

Ὀψίας δὲ γενομένης, προσῆλθον αὐτῷ οἱ μαθηταὶ
Opsias de genomenis, prosilthon auto oi mathitai
Evening however coming, came near to Him the disciples

αὐτοῦ, λέγοντες Ἔρημός ἐστιν ὁ τόπος, καὶ ἡ ὥρα
autou, legontes Erimos estin o topos, kai i ora
of Him, saying Desert is the place, and the hour

ἤδη παρῆλθεν· Ἀπόλυσον τοὺς ὄχλους, ἵνα ἀπελθόντες
idi parilthen. Apoluson tous ochlous ina apelthontes
already is gone by. Dismiss the crowds that going away

εἰς τὰς κώμας ἀγοράσωσιν ἑαυτοῖς βρώματα.
eis tas komas agorasosin eautois vromata.
into the villages they may buy for themselves foods.

Ὁ δὲ Ἰησοῦς εἶπεν αὐτοῖς, Οὐ χρείαν ἔχουσιν
O de Iisous eipen autois, Ou chreian echousin
But Jesus said to them, Not need they have

ἀπελθεῖν· δότε αὐτοῖς ὑμεῖς φαγεῖν.
apelthein; dote autois ymeis fagein.
to go away; give to them you to eat.

Οι δὲ λέγουσιν αὐτῷ, Οὐκ ἔχομεν ὧδε εἰ μὴ πέντε ἄρτους
Oi de legousin auto Ouk echomen ode ei mi pente artous
But say to Him Not we have here except five loaves

καὶ δύο ἰχθύας. Ὁ δέ εἶπε Φέρετέ μοι αὐτοὺς ὧδε.
kai duo ichthuas. O de eipe Ferete moi autous ode.
and two fish. He however said Bear to me them here.

Καὶ   κελεύσας   τοὺς ὄχλους ἀνακλιθῆναι ἐπὶ τοὺς χόρτους,
Kai kelefsas tous ochlous anaklithinai epi tou chortous,
And commanding the crowds to recline on the   grass,

καὶ λαβὼν τοὺς πέντε ἄρτους καὶ τοὺς δύο ἰχθύας,
kai lavon tous pente artous kai tous duo ichthuas,
and taking the five   loaves and the   two   fishes,

ἀναβλέψας εἰς τὸν οὐρανὸν, εὐλόγησε καὶ κλάσας
anavlepsas eis ton ouranon, evlogise   kai klasas
looking up to   the Heaven, He blessed and broke

ἔδωκε τοῖς μαθηταῖς τοὺς ἄρτους,   οἱ δὲ μαθηταὶ τοῖς
edoke tois mathitais tous artous, oi de mathitai tois
He gave to the disciples the loaves, and the disciples to the

ὄχλοις,   καὶ ἔφαγον πάντες, καὶ ἐχορτάσθησαν·
ochlois,   kai efagon pantes, kai echortasthisan;
crowds, and   ate   all,   and were satisfied;

καὶ   ἦραν   τὸ περισσεῦον τῶν κλασμάτων,
kai   iran   to perisseuon ton klasmaton,
and they took the excess   of the fragments,

δώδεκα   κοφίνους   πλήρεις.
dodeka   kopfinous   plireis.
twelve   handbaskets   full.

THE GATE

Beyond the gate,
The garden gate
Fixed among the creepers
Vesseling the back stone wall,
Beyond, through tangled weeds and saplings,
Through beds of nettles and opaque thickets
Lining the periphery . . .

Just beyond the threshold
Of that you now call home—
That which you have walked and rewalked,
Pruned and proliferated—
In the back,

Deep in the haze,
Behind the rows and spaces,

Where the growth presses in
Upon the lattice of the gate,
The inflection point . . .

Toward this we grow
Blessed heliotropes,
Distant in the drone of leaves,
Far-faced children,
With deep miasma eyes
And endless sighs,
Who work so hard, so long,
Our voices echoing
Like the vast engines of night trains
Hurtling through unchecked space,
Never knowing yet one blink,
A nudge of the latch,
And we are through—
There I will be.

You know me.

I am a world
Of unspeakable peace and security,
Indescribable beauty,

Pleasure that passeth understanding.
I am a world where worries over
Work, money, conflict
Are but a distant dream,
Things seldom recalled.

I am a world where all lost loves are found,
Where the heart settles in,
Where we gather all at last,
Together, laughing,
Feasting at the banquet of the great reunion
The great wedding,
On the first warm afternoon of spring,
Perpetual.

You think you almost see me now
Sometimes,
Never realizing
There I am,
Always clear before you
In the twilight
Of the brilliant here and now.

THE
INFLECTION
POINT

They say the sky is bigger in Colorado. It's true. The mountains produce this effect. They provide the otherwise featureless infinity of the sky with a scale, a sense of dimension not found on the flatlands.

As my eyes followed the chain of massive peaks north along the Front Range, the mountains became invisible in the glare. I sighed. It was a gorgeous summer solstice in Colorado. The winds were soft, the skies clear as glass, and there were no signs of an incoming front. After a long winter's wait, finally, conditions were perfect to camp high in the mountains.

. . .

I loaded the car with backpacking equipment and three enthusiastic golden retrievers. Threading my way along the dizzying gravel switchbacks that wound up the back side of the mountain, I arrived at the pass at 11,200 feet. Parking several hundred feet below the ridge, I hiked a steep trail through flowering alpine tundra to the very top of the divide and pitched the tent.

The view was spectacular in the summer dusk. To the west, an array of mountain ranges receded blue into blue until the eye lost track, the mind unable to interpret the distances, the impossible perspective arrayed before it. To the east lay the cities of Boulder and Denver, their billion points of light gleaming in microscopic splendor, a vast sea of prairie rolling away behind them in the haze for hundreds of miles.

Such is the vantage point of the Continental Divide. Here all precipitation landing on the eastern side of the ridge flows east to Boulder Creek and eventually makes its way to the Atlantic Ocean. All precipitation falling on the western side of the ridge flows down to the Colorado River, eventually emptying into the Pacific Ocean.

I needed water to prepare my camp food. The snow-covered cap of a small glacier lay only a few feet away. I scooped handfuls of granular summer snow into a pan and began to melt it with my propane stove. As I swirled the slurry gently, a few ounces suddenly sloshed over the rim and landed on a sharp piece of granite at my feet. As I continued to heat the remaining water, I contemplated the tiny rivulets that ran down the edges of the stone with fascination. In theory, the drops that landed on the eastern side of the rock would end up in the Atlantic Ocean, while the drops that landed on the other side would end up in the Pacific Ocean. Although hard to believe, the difference of a fraction of an inch here at the point of origin would eventually result in the difference of an entire ocean—an entire world.

It's funny, but that's how cause and effect is: The difference in one step, one choice, one word, one little thought form at the point of origin can make a literal world of difference as the flow sweeps us downstream, inexorably amplifying our intent.

Although you may not realize it, you are balanced on your own Continental Divide every moment of your life. Each second of your life, you walk along a precipitous ridge, a knife edge that divides your life into two entirely different potential dimensions. On one side lies the world you live in now, the world of ordinary struggle and uncertainty. On the other side, stretching away in all its majesty, lies the world of self-empowerment, the world of self-creation—the dimension of the miraculous, where dreams unfold with perfect precision.

On this side lies heaven.

Each moment as you walk this ridge that is your life, you make a choice. Whether you are aware of it or not, each moment you choose to pour the water of your thoughts down one side or the other. You either choose to sow thoughts of uncertainty, conflict, and lack, or you choose to sow thoughts of fulfillment, happiness, and ease—visions of intentional, positive creation.

In the most practical sense possible, you choose each second to remain either in the dimension of the ordinary or to enter the dimension of the miraculous. And, as you continue walking the razor's edge of your existence, the thoughts you sow flow down the sides of the great slopes of cause and effect, gaining momentum, snowballing, expanding, until they inevitably crest at the critical threshold of manifestation and become the personal reality you see around you.

THE ANCIENT MOTIF

It makes a great story. In fact, it follows a motif used by storytellers for eons; a plot that reappears perennially and is found yet today in hit movies and bestselling books. It goes something like this: There is strife, trouble, a great need. A secret document is found—it could be a treasure map, a lost formula or text, instructions for a special ritual, or perhaps directions to an ancient tomb laden with fabulous riches.

The document is ancient, enigmatic, and mysterious. The message it carries is difficult to unravel but is finally deciphered. Ultimately, as the story progresses, the directions within the document are followed, and a miraculous discovery is made. Great wealth or power or good fortune are finally achieved. The protagonist's problems are solved and everyone lives happily ever after.

Like I say, it makes a great story. But when this motif actually unfolds before you in your life, it's even better.

What would you say if I were to tell you that I can show you a real secret document, a real treasure map? In keeping with the motif, this document is ancient—

hidden away for years. It is enigmatic and mysterious. It is a kind of map which, if followed carefully, can lead you to a great treasure, to a new world filled with incredible people, places, and things. It can lead you to riches—real riches—beyond your wildest dreams.

As a reasonable person, you may question that such a document exists. You will say that finding such a document can't happen to real people living in the real world. In fact, if you did not express this kind of reasonable skepticism, I would be disappointed. For such a reaction is normal, the mark of someone who is thinking clearly. Nonetheless, as the book unfolds, I think you will find that the words do, in fact, reveal a real treasure: the technique of miracles, the Philosopher's Stone, the catalyst sought throughout the ages that transmutes base into gold, darkness into light, and suffering into joy.

THE HIDDEN MONOLITH

In the late Stanley Kubrick's landmark movie, *2001*, explorers on the far side of the moon find an enigmatic black monolith buried curiously beneath the surface. Eventually, this mysterious object turns out to be a door, a stargate leading to a higher dimension. The unspoken implication is that the featureless rectangle was placed on the moon—rather than Earth—deliberately, so that it could not be found by human beings until we had reached a sufficiently advanced state of evolution, until we were able to handle the power contained within.

Obviously, the monolith is a metaphor, a symbol that represents higher knowledge, knowledge that unlocks an entirely new realm of wisdom and light. It is a very appropriate metaphor as well, for as the world now actually begins a new millennium, we are each finding our own monoliths, our own stargates that will enable us to enter new dimensions of understanding and personal power.

The powerful document revealed in this book—a text I call the "Alpha Passage"—has been just such a gate for me. As you study it carefully and follow its directions, I feel certain it will become just such a gate for you as well.

I have always wondered: Did Spirit somehow intend this passage to remain encrypted? Was it for the same reason the monolith was hidden in the movie? If made too obvious, would it have fallen into our hands too early to be used effectively—and responsibly?

THE ALPHA PASSAGE

The Alpha Passage is hidden in such an obvious place that it has been overlooked. It lies within a well-known section of the gospel of Matthew. There, the author of the original composition has embedded a subtext within the subtleties of the ancient and extraordinarily complex words of the original Greek.

In this subtext, the technique of miracles is laid out in twelve steps, twelve conditions. When these twelve *conditions* are activated, they act as a kind of combination lock, opening a gate leading to the dimension of the miraculous. Using standard reference books, this book will show you word for word how the technique has been encoded within the original text.

You may be surprised to learn that you are already working with many of these conditions and are familiar with the concepts behind them. Once you see them laid out all together in an organized fashion, you will finally be able to put all the pieces together. Once assembled, these conditions function like an engine with twelve cylinders. When all twelve cylinders fire together, the power they generate is beyond comprehension. It is a power that can change your life so drastically that you cannot—in your current state of evolution—

imagine the universe that will open for you. You will see that you have the power to manifest heaven in your life here and now.

THE NEANDERTHAL ECLIPSE

Miracles are poorly understood. Often we think of them as events in which the laws of the universe, the laws of cause and effect, are somehow circumvented. A miracle occurs when something "impossible" happens. We believe this about miraculous events only because we fail to understand the processes of cause and effect that enable them. We are very much like Neanderthals observing an eclipse. Because we lack the proper knowledge, we rationalize what we observe in peculiar, supernatural terms when, in fact, what transpires has an entirely natural explanation.

Consider: If we did not understand the genetic and bio-chemical fundamentals of life, we would think the simple germination of a seed was somehow supernatural as well. But we understand that for a seed to germinate, certain conditions must be present: a viable seed, moisture, warmth, soil, oxygen, carbon dioxide, nitrogen, trace elements, alternating darkness and light, the proper pH, and time.

When all of these conditions are established simultaneously, the cellular machinery of the dormant seed is activated; it begins to absorb and organize the raw materials around it, and growth occurs. In time, as the conditions are maintained, the seedling matures into an enormous tree, which bears tremendous quantities of fruit. The process is a "miracle" certainly, yet it follows natural sequences of cause and effect.

MULTIPLE DIMENSIONS IN A QUANTUM WORLD

Recent advances in fields such as physics and medicine have shattered the boundaries of what scientists previously thought possible. Even the concept of "parallel universes"—two universes existing side by side—is obsolete in the new millennium. It's all so much bigger than we ever thought.

In 1956, Huge Everett III, a Ph.D. candidate in physics at Princeton University, proposed what is known as the "Many Worlds Hypothesis" in his now famous doctoral thesis. This idea states that there are not only multiple dimensions, multiple universes, but an *infinite* number of them. Everything that can be, everything that is *possible*, eventually becomes real somewhere in some universe.

Considered irrational and extreme by many when first proposed, this idea has long since become a part of mainstream scientific thought. A majority of physicists currently believe that the Many Worlds Hypothesis—or some variation thereof—is the only rational way to explain what is being observed in cutting-edge experimental physics.

Consider the following statements in *Scientific American*, May 2003, regarding the Many Worlds Hypothesis: "It predicts that one classical reality gradually splits into superpositions of many such realities—observers experiencing this splitting merely as a slight randomness . . . The act of making a decision causes [a] person to split into multiple copies." Note carefully the cause-and-effect sequence: A new universe is formed *because* you make a conscious decision—a new and separate reality branching out from all the others in *response* to your thoughts.

Is it not astonishing? Physicists arriving at the same conclusion reached long ago by metaphysicians: *Form follows thought.*

The universe rearranges itself
around our states of consciousness.

THE DEMONSTRATION
AND THE DEMONSTRATOR

Several years ago, a series of unusual events led me to begin studying the account of the Miracle of the Loaves and Fishes in the gospel of Matthew (14:13–23). Scholars have long suspected there was something unique about the Miracle of the Loaves and Fishes. Of all the miracles attributed to the man known in the Bible as Jesus of Nazareth, this is the only one included in all four gospels.

Further, it is a miracle that Jesus, as the demonstrator, performed not once but twice—on another occasion four thousand people were fed in much the same manner (Matt. 15:32–39). It was as if the demonstrator of the miracle were saying, "Watch carefully and make no mistake. I will show this carefully for all to see, and repeat it—so that you will see how to do this for yourselves."

And would we not expect this? The demonstrator, and others like him, have always said that others "would do even greater things." It is logical that a master miracle worker would perform the miracle and make a special point of showing us *how* to do it ourselves. Every wise person knows that it is good to feed a hungry person a fish but far better to show the person how to fish. Would we not expect to find a lesson somewhere in the teachings that gives specific instructions for the technique of manifestation that is demonstrated so well on this and other occasions?

With this in mind, I looked hard at the words in Matthew's account and thought about them for days. But as I studied the miracle carefully, I found few clues as to the method behind the miracle. The standard King James Version seems little more than a sketchy description:

13 *When Jesus heard of it, he departed thence by ship into a desert place apart: and when the people had heard thereof, they followed him on foot out of the cities.*

14 *And Jesus went forth, and saw a great multitude, and was filled with pity toward them, and he healed their sick.*

15 *And when it was evening, his disciples came to him, saying, This is a desert place, and the time is now past; send the multitude away, that they may go into the villages, and buy themselves victuals.*

16 *But Jesus said unto them, They need not depart; give ye them to eat.*

17 *And they say unto him, We have here but five loaves, and two fishes.*

18 *He said, Bring them hither to me.*

19 *And he commanded the multitude to sit down on the grass,*

and took the five loaves, and the two fishes, and looking up to heaven, he blessed, and brake, and gave the loaves to his disciples, and the disciples to the multitude.

20 And they did all eat, and were filled: and they took up of the fragments that remained twelve baskets full.

21 And they that had eaten were about five thousand men, beside women and children.

22 And straightaway Jesus constrained his disciples to get into a ship, and to go before him unto the other side, while he sent the multitudes away.

23 And when he had sent the multitudes away, he went up into a mountain apart to pray: and when the evening was come, he was there alone.

Poring over these words, I felt as though I had reached a barrier. Nothing conclusive was gained. Then came my big break: In a final attempt to glean all possible information contained within the text, I began to translate the passage for myself using the original Greek words which the author of Matthew used to craft the manuscript.

It was a fascinating and somewhat frustrating process, for Greek does not translate readily into English. In fact, it would be accurate to say that translating Greek is a rather tricky and difficult matter, requiring careful attention to detail, as well as deference and respect for the original author's intent.

Greek is a particularly deep and complex language. It is the language of one of the most sophisticated cultures in history, a language developed and used by philosophical geniuses like Plato and Socrates and Aristotle. It is the language of an ancient civilization—and a way of *thinking* —separated from us in time by thousands of years. The words of this ancient language can contain multiple layers of highly subtle innuendo. Even trained scholars struggle over translation details.

To better grasp this critical point, consider the first phrase in the first sentence of the gospel of John, which is traditionally translated, "In the beginning was the Word . . ." If you research this phrase, you will find that the original Greek says "In the beginning was the *logos.*" Although traditional translations such as the *King James Version* contain no hint whatsoever of the depth of the term *logos,* a quick look at a standard Greek to English dictionary—such as the one found in *Strong's Exhaustive Concordance*—reveals the following:

logos, log'-os; from *3004;* something *said* (including the *thought*); by implication a *topic* (subject of discourse),

also *reasoning* (the mental faculty) or *motive;* by exten-
sion a *computation;* specifically (with the art. in John) the
Divine *Expression* (i.e. *Christ*):——account, cause, commu-
nication, X concerning, doctrine, fame, X have to do,
intent, matter, mouth, preaching, question, reason, +
reckon, remove, say (-ing), shew, X speaker, speech,
talk, thing, + none of these things move me, tidings,
treatise, utterance, word, work.*

It is interesting to note that the term "word" is listed at
the very end of this maze of complex information, almost as
an afterthought. And yet for reasons that are entirely unclear,
medieval scholars somehow deemed it appropriate to "sim-
plify" translation to this single term.

Now, as confusing and ambiguous as the information in
Strong's Exhaustive Concordance may be, things only become
more complicated with deeper study. If you look up the term
logos in Mircea Eliade's *Encyclopedia of Religion and Philosophy,*
another standard reference found in many libraries, you will
find that there are a full *twelve pages* devoted to this term.

At its most superficial level, *logos* can refer to a spoken or

---

Strong's Exhaustive Concordance of the Bible by James Strong, S.T.D., LL.D, Holman Bible
Publishers, 1982.

written word. But more important, *logos* refers to that which gives rise to words which is, of course, thought. Further, *logos* can refer to the creative cause-and-effect relationship between thoughts and words and, more generally, to the creative power of thoughts to manifest events and circumstances.

Logos was a critical philosophical term used six hundred years before the advent of Christianity by the philosopher Heraclitis. Heraclitis believed that all that manifested in the universe was the direct result of interactions between the great opposites, light and dark, male and female, hot and cold—an ideology strikingly similar to Taoism. The way in which Heraclitis defined *logos* was incorporated into the substrate of the Greek language. Subsequent use of this term was never completely free of his influence. John almost certainly knew this when writing his gospel.

Thus, the phrase in John could be better translated, "In the beginning was a thought with powerful potential, a creative intent that ultimately gave rise to the entire universe." But in the standard biblical translation, you have been told only that *logos* means "word." Can you begin to see how much you might be missing as you read other passages in standard translations?

As you will find in the pages that follow, the same depth applies to many of the terms Matthew used to write the Alpha Passage. As we dissect and study these terms carefully in the following pages, I am confident you will agree that the Alpha Passage contains a wealth of information on the actual technique used to set up and enact the miracle. This is information that is highly practical, information that you can begin to use *now* to enact your own miracle and enter the dimension of heaven.

EMPTINESS

Καὶ ἀκούσας ὁ Ἰησοῦς ἀνεχώρησεν   ἐκεῖθεν   ἐν
Kai akousas o Iisous anechorisen   ekeithen   en
And hearing   Jesus   withdrew   from there   in

πλοίῳ εἰς   ἔρημον τόπον κατ᾽ ἰδίαν καὶ   ἀκούσαντες
ploio   eis   eremon topon kat idian kai   akousantes
a boat into a desert place privately and having heard

οἱ ὄχλοι   ἠκολούθησαν αὐτῷ πεζῇ   ἀπὸ τῶν πόλεων.
oi ochloi ikolouthisan auto   pezi   apo ton poleon.
the crowd   followed   Him on foot from the cities.

At first glance, the initial sentence of the Alpha Passage may appear to be nothing more than a routine introductory statement that says, "Before the important events of the day took place, Jesus happened to travel into the desert."

Nothing could be farther from the truth. To see why, let's look more closely at the statement. It is in no way casual. Rather, it clearly reveals the first critical condition that must *always* initiate a miraculous event.

Think about it: What is a desert really? What is the true nature, the *essence,* of such a place? A desert is an unusual environment because it is virtually devoid of any substantial resources. A desert has no food, no water, no shelter, and no edible vegetation. But more important, a desert has no people, no politics, no arguments, no books, and—no words. A desert is a place of profound isolation, silence, and *emptiness.*

In essence, when Jesus went into the desert, he situated himself within what might be referred to as a vacuum.

A vacuum is a very special situation. Because it is empty, it possesses the tremendous potential to be filled. Like a magnet, a vacuum exerts a force that pulls things inexorably toward it. The less a vacuum contains—the emptier it is— the more powerful the attractive force it exerts on the surrounding world.

Consider for a moment what it would be like to be within a vacuum. Image that you are sitting somewhere and all the air, all the matter, all the energy, all the light immediately surrounding you is taken away. What kind of things would you observe from this vantage point? Observing the world around you while situated within a vacuum, you would see something very interesting: You would see everything rushing toward you. You would see energy and resources automatically flowing toward you from every direction. Why? Because of a principle that everyone knows: Nature abhors a vacuum. Whenever a state of emptiness or lack is created, nature immediately mobilizes to fill it.

And what is Nature? There should be no confusion on this point: Nature is Spirit, or at least a very large part of Spirit. Therefore, another way of stating this law is that

Spirit abhors a vacuum.

A vacuum is a state, a condition. When carefully analyzed, any miracle can be shown to begin with this condition. Consider the greatest of all miracles—the creation of the universe itself. Before anything came into being, perfect emptiness existed—there was no space, no time, and no matter. The intelligent creative force that underlies all things was not satisfied with that emptiness and set about to fill it. In other words, Spirit filled the void with the universe, which is still expanding with incredible force in every direction.

The Miracle of the Loaves and Fishes begins in the same way. By going into the desert, the demonstrator established himself within a vacuum, thereby setting into motion powerful and automatic forces that began to alter the processes of flow around him. Using the original Greek, let's look carefully at the exact words in Matthew's description:

Iisous anechorisen ekeithen en ploio
eis eremon topon kat idian.

Here are the translations of the key words in this phrase according to *Strong's Exhaustive Concordance:*

- *Iisous* is the Greek name for Jesus.
- *Anechorisen* can mean "to depart," as the traditional translation indicates—this is clearly one of the word's meanings. But *anechorisen* can also be used to mean "to withdraw the self." In contemporary psychological terms, we could quite accurately substitute the word "ego" for self. The definition then becomes "to withdraw the ego."
- *Topon* can refer simply to "a place"; this is true. But it

is critical to note from *Strong's Exhaustive Concordance*
that this word can also refer to a "condition" or "opportunity"—in other words, a place of *potential*.

- *Kat* means "down."
- *Eremon* can refer to a "desert" but can also indicate,
  more generically, "an empty or solitary place."
- *Idian* can indeed be translated as "privately." But
  Strong's Exhaustive Concordance tells us *idian* can also
  be translated as "pertaining to the self."

Now, using this straightforward information—obtained
directly from a universally accepted reference dictionary—
we can easily translate the passage in a new way. This translation reveals a deeper, richer, and far more *useful* level of
information:

*Jesus went away into the desert, alone. There he withdrew his
self, or ego, by going down into a state of emptiness and inner
stillness—a place or "condition" of potential.*

It is fascinating to note that Jesus didn't just go alone into
the desert *before* the miracle took place. Verse 22–23 tells us
that he went *back* into the desert after the miracle was con-
cluded:

And straightaway Jesus constrained his disciples to get
   into a ship, and to go before him unto the other side,
   while he sent the multitudes away.
And when he had sent the multitudes away, he went up
   into a mountain apart to pray: and when the evening
   was come, he was there alone.

In other words, the demonstrator started from a place of
emptiness and silence and, once completed, *returned* to a
place of emptiness and silence. As we will see, one of the
concepts that surfaces over and over in our study of the miracle is that of *circularity*. For a miracle worker, the conditions
of a miracle are sequenced like the chambers of a powerful
combustion engine: They move through a series of *cycles*.
These cycles enable a miracle worker to consistently and re-
liably manifest what is needed and beneficial.

In this universe, the true power—the great flow that
brings life and energy and lavish abundance—travels in a
moving circle, a spiral. This dynamic spiral constantly returns
to a new starting point, recharged and primed for another
powerful flow of good. Miracle workers understand this circularity at a deep level. They move *with* this flow. They work
with the great cycle—never against it—and in doing so harness its extraordinary power for the good.

THE TRAGEDY

This information will now allow you to understand an extremely important event that transpired the day before the miracle was demonstrated. This critical event, a tragedy of the highest order, is not normally thought to be connected to the miracle. In truth, it was an integral part of the process of cause and effect that led to the great demonstration of abundance.

Do you recall the terrifying story that immediately precedes the Alpha Passage? It is an account of how the miracle worker's great mentor, friend, and forerunner—the man he admired most in all the world—was not only taken from him but taken in the most horrifying and sickening way possible. The day before the miracle was the day that Herod had John the Baptist beheaded and his head delivered to his court on a platter. This for no better reason than to pacify Herodias, the mother of the young girl with whom he was having an affair.

There is nothing anywhere in the narrative to indicate how Jesus reacted to this. The fine art of describing how people felt internally was not incorporated into writing until centuries later. We are simply told that just before the miracle occurred, Jesus was told of his unfathomable loss, and that when he heard of it he went alone into the desert.

Imagine that you are an extremely unusual person—so unusual that you have only one other person in the whole world that you can relate to as a teacher and friend. Imagine how much this person would mean to you. Now, if it is possible, try to imagine how incredibly lonely, how grief stricken, how *empty* you would be to learn that this special friend— your lifeline to humanity—was suddenly gone from your life.

Nothing happens by accident, certainly nothing in the life of an enlightened being who is about to trigger an event that will inspire billions of people for millennia. The *timing* of John's death is critical.

Remember that we said the emptier a vacuum, the more *powerful* its ability to attract? What bigger vacuum could possibly have been created in the life of Jesus? Only the death of his mother, or perhaps Mary Magdalene, his other close friend and confidant, could have produced the profound loss that he experienced.

But the enlightened don't cave in to setbacks. It is one of their hallmarks.

It is said that you can judge the true depth of a saint's enlightenment by watching how long it takes him or her to recover from a terrible blow. Ordinary people may take many long months or years to snap back from a major setback. By contrast, when put to the test, the truly enlightened snap back in hours or days.

Such was the case with Jesus. Neither loss, lack, or adversity could ever keep him from generating positive changes. In fact, quite the opposite is true. As is the case with all advanced beings, Jesus had the ability to use loss as a *fuel,* as a kind of raw material to stoke the engines of transmutation.

The enlightened are, in essence, processing plants, energy centers that constantly transmute. They constantly convert everything around them from the negative into the positive, everything dark and ignorant into light and knowledge. And, consciously or unconsciously, the *way* they accomplish this is by setting up and maintaining the twelve conditions.

PUTTING EMPTINESS
TO WORK IN YOUR LIFE

Translating these passages, learning about the power of emptiness and the other conditions of a miracle, is not a mere intellectual exercise. The information contained within the words you are contemplating has immense practical value. It is critical for you to learn exactly how you can work with these concepts, how you can *apply* this knowledge to your own particular situation. You cannot simply read about what happened. You have to act.

Just how can you "go into the desert," set up a vacuum, and so put yourself in a position to experience good things flowing toward you? This must be accomplished on two different levels—the internal and the external.

Internally, "going into the desert" means going to a place deep within and emptying the mind of thoughts. The expanded translation discussed at the beginning of this chapter makes this clear. Making the effort to suspend your internal dialogue is a critical step in activating the first condition of a miracle.

Jesus, like most other holy men and women, often sought isolated places such as deserts and mountaintops. And why do the enlightened covet silence? It is not so much because silence helps them to think more clearly but because silence enables them *not* to think.

The constant clamor and commotion of thoughts block the still, small, subtle voice of Spirit. All enlightened individuals are acutely aware of this and are experts at quieting their minds so that they can hear clearly.

It is common knowledge that the demonstrator sought deserted places so that he could pray and meditate. And what is meditation but the process of descending into the self, beneath the stream of superficial thoughts, to that place of stillness where the mind of God, with all its infinite information, is freely accessible.

> *There he withdrew his self, or ego, by going down into a state of emptiness and inner stillness—a place or "condition" of potential.*

MEDITATION FOR THE MIRACLE WORKER

It is easy to forget that we have an unlimited field of intelligence resting within us like a deep and quiet pool. We cannot see this because our tightly woven thoughts, like a dense bank of clouds, block our perception of the infinite wellspring of consciousness within.

Like clouds, our thoughts have little substance. Though fleeting and diaphanous, they nonetheless can block the light very effectively when they hang between the sun and us. Mystics and contemplatives from every spiritual tradition have recognized this for thousands of years.

For example, the inspirational classic *The Cloud of Unknowing*, written anonymously by a fourteenth-century mystic, teaches that our ideas about the way the universe operates are so limited they keep us from knowing the greater truth. The author teaches that our fearful, rigidly bound perceptions and logical thoughts actually blind us to the enormity of the Creator's true nature and true potential. True knowledge, according to *The Cloud of Unknowing*, can only be obtained by silencing all conscious thought, by consistently checking all attempts to perceive or understand the Infinite with words and logic:

> *When you are alone in prayer, let go all thoughts—whether good or bad—and attend only to the present moment. . . . Do everything to behave as if you did not know that your memories and thoughts press between you and God. Try to look over their shoulders, seeking something else, which is God shrouded in the cloud of unknowing.*

Meditation is the process of shifting awareness from thoughts to the breaks between thoughts. With patience, practice, and persistence, the empty spaces between thoughts inexorably widen until the spaces are greater than the thoughts themselves. *This establishes a vacuum at the spiritual and mental level.*

When you have attained this state of inner stillness, even partially, you can immediately begin tapping the fountainhead of intelligence and draw on its indescribable power.

The ability to access this meditative state is vital to the success of *your* dream, *your* miracle. Within it is knowledge, and knowledge is power. And it is power—the right kind of spiritual power—that will allow you to *change* things.

This knowledge, this power, will come in large part, in the form of *information.*

Anyone seeking to correct a state of lack needs information. But the right kind of information may be unavailable at the conscious level. For the most part, conscious thoughts do little more than confuse the issue. To paraphrase the writer Arnold Patent:

> *The conscious mind has only one truly useful function,*
> *and that is to make the decision to turn itself off.*

The information that can really help you manifest your dreams is found at a much deeper stratum than conscious thought. The information that will lead you to the fulfillment of your dream lies waiting for you in the realm of the intuitive or subconscious mind. The knowledge you find here is the kind of knowledge that allows you to inexplicably know what to do or what to say or where to be. This is the kind of knowledge that allows you to have perfect timing and synchronicity.

Miracles unfold not by magic but by knowledge. Money will not "magically" appear in your wallet. The perfect job will not be thrust upon you as you sit idly on your couch. A soul mate will not materialize from thin air and ring your doorbell. Disease will not inexplicably heal as you continue to think negative thoughts and abuse your body. Instead you will *learn* how to make your miracle real. You will *learn* how to make money. You will come to *understand* how to go about curing the disease, where to look for your job or your soulmate.

ACHIEVING STILLNESS

Perfect stillness of the mind is difficult but not impossible to achieve. Like most truly enlightened people, the Nazarene was a master of perfect stillness. That is why he could say with conviction, "I and the Father are one."

In the West, Christian mystics call the state of perfect stillness "Christ Consciousness." In the East, this state is commonly referred to as *samadhi*. Other cultures and traditions use other terms, but they all mean the same thing. The heightened state of awareness and the knowledge you can achieve through meditation will give your life tremendous power. When the activity of the conscious mind or ego becomes perfectly quiet, the full energy and light of the One pours through the self unobstructed.

When this happens, miracles happen spontaneously as you find yourself automatically at the right place at the right time learning and doing the right things. This is why, when your miracle finally manifests—and it *will* manifest if you consistently establish the twelve conditions—the process by which it manifests will seem effortless and the *solution* obvious.

If you don't know how to meditate, get a book or an audio program about it. Consider learning Transcendental Meditation or Zen meditation or yoga. Many Eastern religions have superb techniques for meditating. If you are so inclined, you can also ask your priest, minister, rabbi, or a knowledgeable friend about Judaeo-Christian meditation techniques.

THE EXTERNAL VACUUM

As indicated, emptiness must be established both internally and externally. Meditation creates a vacuum within the self, but you will also have to create a state of emptiness in the world around you in order to finish setting up the first condition of a miracle.

Here's how this works: Often when people suffer lack, they cling more fiercely to what they have, not realizing this staunches the flow of good into their life. A classic example is a person experiencing financial difficulties. She balances her checkbook and each month sees that she is having increasing difficulty paying the bills. She becomes anxious. She tightens her grip and does everything possible to reduce the flow of money and other resources out of her bank account, out of her life. She dares not let her money flow away and tries to spend less and less. She may even stop giving to charity temporarily, saying, "It's only for a little while. I'll give again and give generously when I have more." She doesn't realize that because everything—including monetary resources—moves in cycles, *nothing* will be coming back around to her if she *releases nothing.*

Look carefully at your own situation. If you are not experiencing complete abundance in every area of your life, you *must* be blocking your flow of incoming energy and resources in some way. The antidote is to release your death grip on your stagnating supply of energy. The temporary "loss" that is created as you begin to give creates a vacuum, which in turn starts to break up the dam. New flow will be stimulated.

THE ANXIOUS FARMER

To help you understand more graphically how a vacuum works in actual practice and how you can begin to create one, consider this simple allegory:

A farmer lived near a beautiful flowing stream that delivered life-giving waters to his crops and livestock as well as to all of the other local farmers. All was well until one early summer when a minor drought caused the stream to run lower than usual. None of the other farmers was worried. They had witnessed many dry spells and accepted them as an inevitable part of nature's normal ebb and flow. They knew that plentiful rains invariably compensate all droughts.

But the worried farmer obsessed and tortured himself. "What if the rains never come again?" he wondered. "If the stream dries up, my crops will wither, my animals will die, and my family will starve." Each anxious thought led to another. He decided there was only one thing to do. He had to accumulate a reserve supply of water to use when the stream eventually dried up. And so, he built a sturdy dam of small boulders and sticks, and in no time a large pond formed. Although the other farmers tried to reason with the misguided man and reassure him, he wouldn't listen. For he had also built a dam deep within himself—a great, impenetrable wall of fear.

The farmers nearby shook their heads. They weren't worried about the farmer trying to withhold all the water. Once full, the force of the stream would carve new channels around the pond, around the anxious farmer's land. And, sure enough, once the pond had filled, the stream reestablished itself on the adjoining neighbor's land. At first the large reserve gave the anxious farmer a feeling of security. But his tendency to worry continued; he had done nothing to correct that. And as he worried on, something happened that he hadn't anticipated: Once the stream had carved new channels that bypassed his pond completely, fresh water no longer flowed into the reservoir.

In the summer heat, the little pond stagnated, and algae bloomed over the surface. Silt and thick weeds choked the bottom. The once abundant fish slowly died, starving for oxygen. As the days went by, the sun beat down upon the pond, and the water slowly evaporated. The anxious farmer watched helplessly as his pond was reduced to a shallow quagmire.

"What will I do?" he moaned. The more he thought, the more confused and anxious he became. At last he set out to find a wise man who lived high in the mountains to the west, a journey of several days. He found the wise man in a simple hut overlooking a magnificent panorama and launched into a long-winded explanation of his problem. The wise man listened patiently. At the end he laughed and told the farmer that the solution was simple. "Tear down the dams," he said, heartily slapping the anxious farmer on the back. "Both of them."

"What do you mean 'both'?" the farmer whined. The wise man's eyes made the farmer very nervous. "I need the water in my pond! It's not much, but it's all I have. If I release it, I will have nothing." But the wise man just turned away and would say no more.

The farmer decided then and there that the so-called "wise man" was insane. The solution he had proposed made absolutely no sense. Upon returning home, however, he realized that unless something changed soon, he would be ruined. The water was so foul now that even the livestock wouldn't drink it. "What have I got to lose?" he asked himself with a shrug.

It was a very good question.

With a sigh of resignation, he walked out to the dam and removed the stones, then watched as the putrid water flowed into the long-dry streambed below. Within an hour, the swamp was completely drained, and the mud beneath began to crack in the hot sun. "Fine. Now I have nothing," he mumbled hopelessly. "How could I have been so stupid?"

In the days that followed, though, the stream above his land began to trickle into the empty, low-lying cavities of the newly drained swamp. In a matter of days, the stream reestablished its old channels, and his problems were solved.

In a strange coincidence, the rains returned about that time, and everyone ended up having a year of great abundance.

If you're experiencing any kind of lack, you are almost certainly making the same mistake as the anxious farmer by clinging desperately in a misguided attempt to conserve what you little you have.

You will have to begin releasing, letting go. Initially, like the farmer, you may feel as though you have made a terrible mistake, but in the process, you will create the kind of emptiness that will automatically pull the flow back into your life. Your actions and your attitude will create a vacuum and energy will begin to flow inexorably toward it—unless, of course, you immediately erect *another* dam of worry and fear.

What do you desire? Examine your situation carefully. Try diligently to see if you have erected a barrier in front of the very thing you want most. This kind of soul-searching regarding the first condition can be applied to any state of lack. For example, if you are experiencing financial problems, are you clinging too fearfully? Do you give enough away to keep the channels of flow open? Do you give *anything* away? If you lack money, release some of what you have. Money was made to circulate, not stagnate.

Create an empty space now to attract the flow of new funds. Understandably, you will be reluctant to make a donation to your favorite charity when you cannot pay your own grocery bill. But sometimes this is the very best thing you can do. You don't have to give a large amount; what is important is that you are willing to release *something* and that you practice releasing *regularly,* and *consistently.*

The same principle can be applied to other forms of lack. If you are starving for a satisfying relationship, you need to honestly ask yourself, "Am I giving freely and openly of myself in my current relationships? Am I generous with my affections, with my time, and with my attention to *everyone* or just a chosen few?" Lack takes many forms, but the basic principle is the same in each case. Your challenge will be to see how this idea applies to your particular problem. Then you must take action. Let me give you a personal example of how this works.

Years ago I was deep in debt from years of medical school and the high cost of setting up my first practice. At that time, I gave nothing to charity in spite of the urging of my wife. I kept telling her we would give later "when our financial situation gets better." But our finances didn't get better. They worsened each month, and I sank into a quagmire of self-pity and despair. At one point I decided to try some positive thinking at my wife's suggestion. I tried visualization and in my mind's eye saw how things could be better. Right away our affairs began to improve a bit. But we soon reached a plateau, and no matter what we did, our situation remained stagnant.

Then, to our horror, we discovered that one of our office workers had embezzled a large sum of money and squandered it on lottery tickets! I was stunned and decided we were doomed, that all our efforts were in vain. Finally things got so bad and the outlook became so hopeless that I hit bottom and surrendered. I just gave up struggling and resisting and doubting and opened myself up, ready to try anything. I was already at rock bottom. What did I have to lose?

It was a very good question.

At that point, I remember that by "coincidence" I came upon a self-help audiotape that detailed how generous giving could stimulate a flow of resources during a phase of stagnation. One night while sitting dejectedly in my office after all the patients had gone home, I decided to try doing what I had just learned on the tape.

Even though I didn't have enough money to pay the rent or the utility bills, I wrote a check for twenty-five dollars to a charity I had always *intended* to support. With a heavy heart I walked to the mailbox and watched as this precious sum disappeared through the slot.

The next morning my receptionist called me out of one of my examination rooms. "Your business insurance agent is on the phone," she reported. "She says it's urgent." I listened in rapt amazement as the agent told me that she had read about the embezzlement in the newspaper. "Your business policy covers the loss," she said. "I'll bring you a check right away for twenty-five hundred dollars."

I was flabbergasted. I didn't even know I *had* a business loss provision in my policy! It was a miracle: Within twelve hours of putting my first check in the mailbox, I received *one hundred times that amount in return.* Sometimes the universe can be very clear.

My life has been on the upswing ever since. I have been consistently committed to charitable giving. By "coincidence" I have always been able to make ends meet.

Activating the First Condition

1. Clarify in your mind what you lack and what you need. Concentrate on the *essence,* not the superficial specifics. Then begin an objective, penetrating examination of your thoughts, attitudes, and behavior. Make sure you understand how you are blocking your own flow by withholding this very thing from the world around you.

2. Begin to calmly release some of your resources. Take it easy. Do not release so much that you strain yourself or cause undue anxiety, but make sure you get the job done. *Relax.* As the flow increases, you can gradually widen the scope of your giving.

3. Cultivate a patient and confident attitude. The dam is made of fear. Do not open the floodgates only to close them once again with anxiety.

4. Be *consistent* and *steady* in your release. This is not a one-time affair. When you release regularly and freely, your flow, your abundance, will be regular and free. This in turn will stimulate you to be ever more consistent, and you will establish a positive, self-fulfilling cycle of good.

5. *Expect* that the flow will sustain itself. *Visualize* the necessary channels opening within your life. Form follows thought.

6. Learn to meditate. Then do it. No miracle will happen if you neglect this step. Once you know how to begin practicing meditation, make time for it and practice regularly. Never let a day go by without meditating.

7. Make a habit of spending time in quiet, solitary places. Forests, mountains, and open spaces contain great energy and power. Surround yourself with this energy and use it to revitalize and recharge yourself as you make your dream come true.

8. Exercise. All the people in the Miracle of the Loaves and Fishes *walked* to the miracle: *And having heard, the*

crowds followed him on foot from the cities. Walking—or any aerobic activity—establishes a kind of vacuum at the cellular level. As the body burns oxygen and glucose, its stores of chemical energy are partially depleted. As anyone who exercises knows, this stimulates the flow of energy and is a powerful way to revitalize.

9. Practice occasional fasting. It is no accident that all of the individuals who experienced the Miracle of the Loaves and Fishes were hungry. Hunger is a powerful state and fasting—controlled hunger—*is an extraordinary and essential tool for all miracle workers.* Mystics from every culture in history have recognized the power of fasting to enable critical breakthroughs in consciousness and flow during periods of uncertainty or stagnation. Fasting has a strong effect on both body and mind, bringing the entire being to a high state of potential.

Jesus lived and trained as an Essene, a fascinating sect that made an elaborate science of fasting. Fasting is at the very core of the Essene way of life. The miracle worker's life clearly indicates he used fasting as one of his most effective tools for creating emptiness and stimulating flow. Learn everything you can about this dynamic technique for correcting lack. *When in doubt, when all else fails to get things moving, try at least a one-day fast. The results will astonish you.*

Fasting is an extraordinarily powerful tool and should be used with great care. Do your fast safely and intelligently. Consult your physician and read *The Master Cleanser* by Stanley Burroughs, available at most health food stores. Also highly recommended is *The Essene Gospel of Peace* translated by Edmond Bordeaux Szekely.

ALIGNMENT

Καὶ   ἐξελθὼν   ὁ Ἰησοῦς   εἶδε   πολὺν   ὄχλον,
Kai   exelthon   o Iisous   eide   polun   ochlon,
And   going out   Jesus   saw   great   a crowd,

καὶ   ἐσπλαγχνίσθη   ἐπ᾽   αὐτούς,   καὶ
kai   esplanchyisthi   ep   autous,   kai
and   was filled with pity   toward   them,   and

ἐθεράπευσε   τοὺς   ἀρρώστους   αὐτῶν.
etherapefse   tous   arrostous   auton.
He healed   the   infirm   of them.

What do you know about the power that moves within this universe? You know that it is vast, certainly. You know that the universe is permeated end to end with unspeakably powerful forces. These forces can shape a billion stars into a galaxy like the Milky Way—100,000 light years in diameter—and keep all of its stars pouring forth unfathomable waves of heat and light and radiation for billions of years.

You know that the power of the universe, the power of nature, can bathe your environment in sunlight, bury it in a ferocious blizzard, or drench it beneath a towering thunderstorm. You know that the universe is so powerful that it can organize atomic and subatomic particles into incredibly complex organic molecules and further organize these into highly intelligent human beings, each with fifty trillion cells, all working together in a perfectly coordinated fashion.

What's more, you have achieved a point of personal evolution in which you know that each iota of energy is precisely interwoven to form a single, intentionally designed tapestry. And you know that if you could only harness an infinitesimal fraction of this endless sea of power you could manifest your dream with perfect precision.

It *is* possible for a human being to accomplish this. You know this, because the great teachers—including the Nazarene—have clearly demonstrated how this can can be utilized. The problem lies with what you *don't* know. For as yet you have only a very vague idea about *how* to harness this energy, *how* to channel it into your life so that you can use it to make your dreams real.

The First Condition shows you how to become aware of the great power—the great river's current—and how to make contact with it by cultivating the right kind of consciousness through meditation. The Second Condition will show you how to further shape your attitudes and actions so that the current will pick you up and carry you efficiently to your desired destination. This is done by a process known as *alignment*.

Alignment is analogous to what a sailor does with a sail boat. The currents of the winds and water surging all around a sailor are constantly changing, very difficult to predict, and totally out of his control. But the sailor has experience on his side. He understands the nature of the currents of wind and water. And he knows precisely how to trim his sails and adjust his rudder so that the current—owever wild and turbulent—carries him exactly where he wants to go.

Right now it may seem as though the great currents of your world are wild and turbulent too. Sometimes the currents carry you in the right direction, but more often it seems as though you are struggling against them—that they are pushing you off your desired course and away from your dream. So often, the great river seems capricious and random, surging this way and that like a bucking horse. You feel so helpless you simply sigh in resignation when things go awry. You shrug your shoulders and say, "That's life. There's no sense fighting it. That's just the way it is." You dejectedly turn your attention back to your daily struggle.

But part of you knows that there is more. Part of you *knows* that you were not born as a child of Spirit to be a helpless victim, blown about haphazardly by random forces. Part of you knows that you are meant to master the art of sailing, that you were meant to soar gracefully like an eagle on the great winds.

THE SHIFT

The next section of the Alpha Passage indicates that when the masses arrived, the demonstrator "came out" of his state of meditation and shifted his focus. He turned his attention from within to without, now focusing on the people surrounding him, feeling their suffering.

The author of Matthew chose a very interesting Greek word to describe the exact nature of this shift from inner to outer focus: *esplanchyisthi*. Although this word is traditionally translated as "filled with pity," a closer examination reveals that a more accurate translation is "moved with compassion." This is key: Matthew doesn't say the demonstrator merely "felt compassion." He chose a word that indicates the demonstrator was *moved* with compassion, *as if being carried by a current.*

Before you can harness the great current and sail upon it, you must, like a good sailor, develop a clear understanding of the nature of the current. What do you know about the current at this point in your journey? Do you think it is random and mindless, governed only by the physical laws delineated so brilliantly by modern scientists? Or is the flowing current intelligent? Does it have a kind of personality, a mindset, a set of higher principles that governs its flow?

Henry Ward Beecher once explained the nature of the great current very succinctly, saying very simply and elegantly, "Love is the river of life in this world." And what is compassion but love in *action,* love in *motion?* Spirit is love, and Spirit is everything—and all things are constantly moving and changing. Everything is *flowing.*

There is no doubt that the terminology used in Matthew was selected with great care and precision. In this section of the Alpha Passage, we are being told that the great current is actually a river of love, and that the way a miracle worker sails its powerful waters is by shifting to a state of compassion. Compassion is a state of consciousness where others' needs and concerns take precedence over all else, even concerns for one's own well being. As such, compassion is the highest manifestation of love.

Think for a moment of exactly what the demonstrator saw when he came out of his state of meditation and beheld the ragged, dusty masses before him. Knowing that he was a highly perceptive and intuitive observer, we can safely assume that he saw the people who milled about him with penetrating accuracy. He saw the people for what they were. He saw all of their human frailties. He not only saw their lack and their hunger, he also saw their spiritual ignorance, their greed, and their selfishness. After all, these were ordinary people with all of the classic human failings.

Put yourself in his position for a moment: What would you feel if you were meditating, dealing with a terrible sense of grief, and you awoke to find a crowd of loud, anxious, haggard individuals pressing in from all sides around you? Do you think you might be somewhat irritated? Would you feel imposed upon, perhaps somewhat offended or disgusted? Almost certainly. But the enlightened react differently than you or me. The passage tells us that the rabbi's *reflex reaction* to what he saw was one of deep concern and care. Far from feeling aggravated, he felt an instantaneous and natural love for the people before him and was automatically moved to begin helping them, to begin doing something.

The wording also says volumes about what he *didn't* feel. He didn't judge the people for their shortcomings or react with revulsion or moral condescension. His compassion contained no political agenda. His compassion was an expression of pure *unconditional* love. We see this again and again throughout his life. The demonstrator clearly made it a practice to seek out the company of the poor, the ignorant, and the diseased—the "sinners" rejected by polite society. We do not generally find him going out of his way to be with the wealthy and powerful, with those who were well fed, well spoken, well dressed, and well educated. Such fortunate individuals had less pressing needs for his services.

If the teacher were alive today, he would probably be working in the inner city, ministering to people with AIDS, counseling gang members, and empathizing with the homeless, mothers on welfare, and criminals. He wouldn't be on talk radio harping about a mean-spirited political agenda. He would not be fearful of different cultures or races. He wouldn't scorn people with different lifestyles or unusual religious beliefs.

The demonstrator would love all people unconditionally. His natural predisposition in any encounter would be to ask:

"How can I help?" not "What's wrong with you?"; "How can I straighten you out?" not "How can I get you to believe what I believe?" The same is true for great holy men and women of every race and creed.

How do you feel about others who appear around you as you travel through your life? It is important to examine your natural reactions to those different from you, those whom you encounter on the street, or in the supermarket as you move through your own life. Be honest with yourself: Do you harbor any subtle disdain for any person or class of people? Do you feel a subtle sense of superiority to any cultural group? Do you look down upon any race or religion or socioeconomic stratum? Do you feel mere "pity," a kind of condescension, when you see someone less fortunate? How often is your automatic reflex reaction one of true, heartfelt compassion? If your honest answer is "not often," then at least you are in touch with the problem.

If you seriously intend to see your dream become reality, then you will need to intentionally cultivate automatic reflexes of genuine compassion. You will have to change your attitudes and reactions—however subtle—from judgment and condemnation to selfless compassion and love if you hope to manifest a miracle.

Think of it this way: Although it may sound odd, *selfless-ness is in your own self-interest*. When you begin to put the welfare of others ahead of your own, your own dreams will begin to advance with incredible efficiency.

THE COMPASSION SHOCK WAVE

Imagine that you take a superb journey overseas. You have three ways in which you can pay for this great experience: You can pay as you go, pay later, or pay ahead of time. This is true with life. So often we "pay" or compensate the universe for our experiences later—as if we were using credit cards. When we elect to pay later, we find ourselves in the awkward position of constantly working to repay energetic debts we have incurred in the past. It is very hard to get ahead like this.

Your life need not be this way. With a little foresight and wisdom, you can start thinking about paying in advance by constantly giving. This can be done very effectively by practicing compassion in all of your affairs, all of your interpersonal relationships. When you pay ahead of time you break down barriers and stumbling blocks *before you even get to them*.

In a sense, paying ahead creates a shock wave in the fabric of cause and effect, a shock wave that travels ahead of you and makes your way clear and easy.

This explains why shifting to a state of compassion enables you to attain synchrony with everything that is going on around you in your world. Since the whole universe is a river of compassion, when you shift to a state of compassion, you become one with the river, one with its vast web of cause and effect.

ONCE YOU ENGAGE IT, DON'T FIGHT THE CURRENT

Imagine that you are stranded in a tiny lifeboat in the middle of the ocean. You drift helplessly in the buffeting waves and currents beneath a relentless sun. Your fresh water and supplies are dangerously depleted. You feel desperate and alone and out of control.

Finally, you catch sight of an island on the horizon. Through your binoculars you see that it is somewhat barren, but from your perspective in the lifeboat it looks like paradise. You pray fervently to be brought safely and quickly to this island. You visualize how great it will be when you arrive;

you think positively; and you repeat numerous affirmations. Above all, you take *action* by rowing with all your might . . .

But the ocean will not cooperate. The swift current carries the lifeboat away from the island. It is too strong to fight. Soon your arms and shoulders burn from the exertion. The oars fall from your blistered hands, and you collapse in despair. You fear you are doomed, but you soon notice that flowing *with* the current is definitely easier than struggling *against* it. Realizing your only hope is to make the best of the situation, you search the horizon for land ahead, in the direction the current is sweeping you.

After a while—and when you least expect it—you suddenly notice something miraculous. You are thrilled and amazed when another island appears. And what a beautiful island it is. As you approach it, you see that it is lush and beautiful, with fruit-bearing trees, freshwater rivers, and rich forests. It is a destination far superior to the barren place you first sighted. You thank God that the current brought you here against your wishes.

Years ago, I experienced something similar in my own life. I once had my heart set on building a house at a specific location. It was very important to me. But no matter how I tried to complete the job, every conceivable thing went wrong. After a prolonged and frustrating struggle, I finally gave up and let go. I felt as though I had failed, as though the universe itself had failed me.

Then something happened. About two months later, my wife and I learned that our intended location had serious problems, problems which would have caused us great expense and hardship for many long years. About that time, while scanning the real-estate market, a new house in an infinitely superior location appeared. We bought it, realizing how close we had come to making a terrible mistake. My family was happier in the new house than we ever thought possible.

Activating the Second Condition

1. With the eyes of Spirit, see the multitudes. Shift your awareness from your own concerns to the concerns of others. At home and at work, be increasingly aware of others' problems and needs.

Pay attention to what's going on in the world, especially to countries and cultures that require aid. If a disaster or problem is brought to your attention, *pay* attention. You may be seeing and hearing something for a reason. Take note. Then *do* something to help. Even doing something small can have a powerful effect on your alignment. The universe will note your intent and respond.

2. Don't limit your compassion to any particular political or cultural group. As an excellent spiritual exercise, try giving some of your attention to those groups you find somewhat offensive. See *all* people as your brothers and sisters, your family.

3. Examine your immediate surroundings. A mistake people often make in practicing compassion is that they focus so much on the big picture that they forget their own microenvironment. This is backwards. You need to *start* with your microenvironment. As the saying goes, "Think globally, act locally." Pay careful attention to the people who surround you most often, your family, coworkers, and friends. Expand outwards only when you have mastered your personal world.

Think of each individual that interfaces with you as a kind of floodgate. Take care that you have carefully opened a channel of compassion with each individual. When you do this, each channel will bring a little more of the flow your way.

4. Fine-tune your synchronicity. This will keep you perfectly aligned with the flow. Pay attention to everything

"mundane" that happens to you throughout the day. If you understand the importance of shifting into compassion, you will find great potential and power in the little things.

Every time you put change into a charity's cannister, let a car move ahead of you in traffic, return your shopping cart to the rack, smile at a stranger, compliment a coworker for good work—every time you do anything unselfish and helpful, you bring yourself closer to *perfect* alignment. Like small adjustments to the rigging of a sailboat, such actions will help you move ahead in all your endeavors with tremendous speed.

5. Heal the sick. Realize that "healing" can take many forms, not all of them at the physical level. Contribute generously to charities that perform this type of service. This will also allow you to release resources and help you establish the First Condition. Purchase food and take it to a local shelter or contribute to charities that feed the poor.

If you are consistently conscious of others' needs, the universe will be consistently conscious of *your* needs. If you consistently help others to prosper, the universe will consistently help you to prosper.

6. Become a lightworker: Consider healing and helping

others by sending them light and love. Several well-designed scientific studies have shown the efficacy of healing prayer.

7. Ask yourself:

What is my mission and my real agenda in wanting fulfillment of this dream?

Where will my dream take me in consciousness?

Will my miracle benefit others or just me?

Will my dream contribute to the universal plan, the higher good?

As I strive for this dream, am I motivated by compassion?

Will the attainment of my dream help me better feel compassion?

Work with these questions until you are very clear about your motives. Evaluate your dream in terms of whether it will harm you or hinder your progress to a state of compassion. Adjust your course—shift your goal so that you are in alignment with the flow of the universe.

Your goal must include the greater good of others. Your success in working miracles will be directly proportional to the care you exercise in this area.

ASKING

Ὀψίας δὲ γενομένης, προσῆλθον αὐτῷ οἱ μαθηταὶ
Opsias de genomenis, prosilthon auto oi mathitai
Evening however coming, came near to Him the disciples

αὐτοῦ, λέγοντες Ἔρημός ἐστιν ὁ τόπος, καὶ ἡ ὥρα
autou, legontes Erimos estin o topos, kai i ora
of Him, saying Desert is the place, and the hour

ἤδη παρῆλθεν· Ἀπόλυσον τοὺς ὄχλους, ἵνα ἀπελθόντες
idi parilthen. Apoluson tous ochlous ina apelthontes
already is gone by. Dismiss the crowds that going away

εἰς τὰς κώμας ἀγοράσωσιν ἑαυτοῖς βρώματα.
eis tas komas agorasosin eautois vromata.
into the villages they may buy for themselves foods.

Ὁ δὲ Ἰησοῦς εἶπεν αὐτοῖς, Οὐ χρείαν ἔχουσιν
O de Iisous eipen autois, Ou chreian echousin
But Jesus said to them, Not need they have

ἀπελθεῖν· δότε αὐτοῖς ὑμεῖς φαγεῖν.
apelthein; dote autois ymeis fagein.
to go away; give to them you to eat.

· · ·

Many years ago when I was young and searching, I was alone and having great difficulty finding someone to share my life with. My situation seemed utterly hopeless, and I had fallen into a state of lonely depression. One night another doctor and I went to see a famous speaker. For some reason, I decided to sit directly in front of him so that I could hear everything he said. The auditorium was packed with over two thousand people, and the room crackled with energy. The lecture was spellbinding.

When he finished the first half of his talk, the speaker asked if anyone had a quick question. He said that he only had time for one or two. At this point, I did something which was very unusual for me. Although I often speak in public and enjoy it greatly, I have always been rather private about my personal life. I rarely discuss my problems with others and *never* before a crowd. But something told me at that moment that I had to make my needs known. I raised my hand.

I told the speaker, in front of the entire auditorium, that I was alone and discouraged because "I couldn't find my soulmate." I was rather long-winded in my explanation. When I was finished, there was a painful silence. I'm sure everyone was thinking the same thing: "How embarrassing! That poor guy. How could he bring this up in front of so many people?"

The great man at the lectern cleared his throat. He responded with classic spiritual ambiguity, saying something general about "letting go" and how "things work out," and closed the meeting for intermission. Although I made every effort to appear unruffled, I was crestfallen. I remember thinking that I had learned nothing helpful, even though I had bared my soul to the world.

Two minutes later, as I stood stupidly in the tightly packed throng that was milling about before the stage, I found myself standing next to a stunningly beautiful woman. I was transfixed. This woman radiated great strength and intelligence and seemed surrounded with light. I struck up a brief and awkward conversation with her, but she remained aloof and appeared to have little interest in me. After a few minutes, she returned to the balcony where she was sitting with friends. I assumed I would never see her again. We were happily married for twenty years.

A similar process of asking occurs in the next phase of the Miracle of the Loaves and Fishes. This section of text indicates that the multitudes made it known to the disciples that they were hungry and needed food. The disciples relayed this information to the demonstrator, who then asked the disciples to feed the crowd. In other words, *information about what was needed was put into words and effectively communicated.* If you want your needs to be fulfilled, you must make them known. You have to ask in order to receive. Formulating an effective and appropriate request for your personal needs will establish the third condition of your miracle.

One of the wisest and most daring requests I know of came from a good friend, Shelley, who lived in rural British Columbia. For years, whenever we would ask her what we could do for her as a friend she would only reply, "Pray for me, see me achieving higher consciousness. That's all I want. That's all that matters."

Shelley always said she didn't care how this was achieved. But she knew exactly what she wanted and wasn't shy about verbalizing it. She was so intent upon her quest that she used an odd device to remind her to stay focused on the goal. She signed her name not with script but with a small figure that had one eye. She was fond of a quote from Matthew 6:22 that summarized her quest for enlightenment: "The light of the body is the eye: if therefore thine eye be single, thy whole body shall be full of light."

One night an astonishing chain of events unfolded which fulfilled her request in a most unusual way. At 11 p.m. she suddenly lost consciousness. When she awoke, she was very confused and had a throbbing headache at the base of her skull. Nausea and diarrhea quickly followed, and she spent a very uncomfortable night at home. The headache persisted. In the morning, her husband insisted she consult a physician. As her condition deteriorated, they drove an hour to the nearest city, where her family practitioner quickly recognized the symptoms of severe neurological disease.

Her pupils were unequal and her optical muscles weren't working properly. An immediate MRI was ordered and their worst fears were realized: Shelley had an enormous aneurysm in a vascular formation called the Circle of Willis at the base of her brain. It was leaking and ready to burst at any moment. The size and location of the aneurysm was so perilous that the neurosurgeon at that hospital pronounced it inoperable. Her death seemed imminent.

As a last resort she was flown to Vancouver, where a world-renowned neurosurgeon agreed to evaluate her. He, too, delivered a very grave prognosis: Her chances were slim at best. To make matters worse, he had no openings in his tightly packed surgical schedule and was leaving in two days for a conference. Other patients, also gravely ill with deadly emergencies, filled every conceivable slot. None of the other surgeons would touch the case.

At the last minute, her miracle began to manifest. An

unusual chain of events suddenly freed an opening in the neurosurgeon's schedule. She underwent a grueling six-hour procedure, in which the time bomb pulsing deep in her brain was somehow defused. Against all odds, and to everyone's amazement, she survived.

The first thing she felt as she woke up in the neurological intensive care unit was that she wanted to "go back." It was all she could think about. She knew that she had been in a place of indescribable peace and wanted to return. She was overwhelmed with the feeling that the other realm was the true reality and that this plane of everyday existence is the dream. As she looked around the intensive care unit, everything was bathed in a deep golden light. The light radiated from every pore of every person and from every object in the room. This perception persisted for many days before it gradually faded away.

But the most important result of her experience was the change that occurred deep inside her. She has never been the same since the operation. Her sense of priorities has completely changed and she no longer worries about material matters. Although she fulfills her everyday responsibilities, she knows at the deepest possible level that mundane details are relatively unimportant. She is firmly centered in the present, deeply contented, and glowing with happiness.

The request she formulated was filled precisely as she

specified. In fact, she now says she needs to be a bit more careful about her requests, for she found just how powerful and accurate they can be: After the aneurysm was repaired, her left eye was disabled for many months. True to her vision, she was left for a time with only one eye.

Another story comes from a close friend who was also involved in a quest for spiritual knowledge. In the 1980s, his interest became so intense that he traveled halfway around the world to study with a great holy man living in an obscure part of India. He learned a great deal, but when he returned home he went through a period of intense questioning and doubt. He wondered if he should keep the holy man as his teacher or move to another discipline altogether.

In the middle of his internal struggle, he was called to his father's deathbed. His father had been ill for some time but was now rapidly deteriorating due to renal failure. The nitrogen in his bloodstream was rising with each passing hour and he had fallen into a deep coma.

Late that night, everyone else left to go home. Only my friend remained, holding solitary vigil at his father's side. At the darkest hour, he fell into a state of deep meditation holding only one question in his mind. He asked Spirit to guide him, to tell him if he should keep his teacher and continue his studies.

As silence rang through the room, his father suddenly lifted his head and opened his eyes. He looked straight at his spellbound son and said, "Keep him." He then fell back into his coma and died, never uttering another word. My friend decided to keep his teacher and experienced countless blessings because of this during the years that followed.

IT'S NOT THE THING, IT'S THE FEELING

It is important to know exactly how to formulate your request. It may seem trivial, but making your needs known to the universe is *no* small matter. If you know what you really want, and how to ask for it, the universe will fulfill your request with startling accuracy. The most crucial concept to keep in mind while formulating requests is: "It's not the thing, it's the feeling."

Our reality, our life, our experience here on Earth is not a series of mere possessions and actions. Life is far deeper and more complex than that. *Personal reality is a series of internal perceptions and feelings.* Therefore, the essence of what we want is never a thing; it is actually an internal experience or a feeling.

All requests should arise from this principle:

Focus on how you want to feel,
not on what thing *you desire.*

It works like this: If you think that what you want is a house, you need to carefully look *beneath* this desire. Make absolutely certain that you know how you want to feel, as well as what you want to experience. If you desire to own a house, for example, are you really looking for the experience of living in the house—for the feelings of security and pleasure the house will allow you to have deep within?

When you formulate your request, make sure you ask for the essence. If you ask directly for the house—and not the spirit that the house will confer—you are putting the cart before the horse. Don't be surprised if this doesn't work. Putting the material before the spiritual can cause serious problems down the line. How many times have you asked for a very specific thing only to find that when you got it, it gave no feeling of satisfaction? If you ask for a very specific house, you might get it only to find that you end up feeling frustrated, confused, and angry.

Conversely, if you start by asking for the feelings of security and pleasure that form the essence of your desire, the universe will supply you with a house that will provide you with a deep sense of fulfillment, joy, and security.

STAYING GENERAL

Always state your request in *general* terms. Resist the temptation to be unduly specific. Let the universe handle the details. Seek the feeling, and let the universe determine the best way to manifest that feeling.

Continuing with the classic example of the house, imagine yourself as a person who has free reign to design a custom-built home. Initially, you are very pleased that you can decide every detail. However, halfway through the building process, it becomes apparent that you don't really know what you are doing. You realize that you don't know how to choose every doorknob and light fixture and molding in order to create a house that will make you happy. In truth, you know virtually nothing about the specifics and you see that it is likely your ill-informed decisions will result in a substandard creation. The end result is a house that is poorly designed with no aesthetic consistency. Your initial excitement evaporates and you feel depressed and cheated.

Now imagine that you go about things differently. This time you wisely formulate your request as follows: "Provide me with shelter which will bring great peace of mind and satisfaction." Instead of trying to do this yourself, you describe the atmosphere and general feel of your dream house to the most experienced master designer you can find. This time the designer handles all of the details, relying on his wisdom and experience. The house that results is extraordinarily beautiful and surpasses even your best expectations. You end up feeling immense pleasure.

Understand that the universe is the master designer. Trust that it will provide for your true needs—without your "help"—and you will end up with a satisfying reality every time.

INTEGRAL NEED

Along with knowing what you really want, it is important to understand what your spirit really needs. When stating your request, you must understand and honor the concept of "integral need." Look again at the Miracle of the Loaves and Fishes. The people in the crowd experienced a miraculous manifestation of food. But they were not present at the site of the miracle with the *intention* of being fed. They were there because they were seeking spiritual knowledge. During the natural course of their search they became hungry. In other words, their hunger was an *integral part* of a far more important purpose.

Never attempt to ask for anything that is not organically connected to such a higher purpose. The universe will have no vested interest in fulfilling a shallow, disconnected need. When you set your course for a disconnected goal, you will automatically veer out of alignment and disengage from the power of the flow.

For example, if you formulate a request for money with no attention to Spirit, you will be on your own. In order for Spirit to supply money in a miraculous way, the need for money has to grow organically as a natural consequence of a Spirit-based endeavor. Seek first the Spirit, *then* all things will be added unto you.

Activating the Third Condition

1. A request must first be put into words. Thoughts, like water vapor, are intangible. In order to make water vapor solid, it must first be condensed into liquid form. Only then can the resultant liquid be frozen into a solid. When manifesting a dream, the first step is to condense the thought forms of your dream into words. This forces you to be very clear about what is desired.

2. Next, put your request in *writing*. Words which are spoken are only the first condensation of thought. Written words take the condensation to another level of solidity. One of the most powerful objects you can ever own is a blank sheet of paper.

Continuously focus on the *essence* of the dream you seek to manifest. What is the spirit beneath the things you desire? What feelings, what experiences are you really hoping to achieve? Make it a habit to ask yourself over and over, "What is it that I *really* want?" Write your description of the essence on a piece of paper, place it in a prominent place, and read it frequently. This will help keep your trajectory true to the mark.

3. Avoid asking directly for money. The disciples proposed to solve the problem of the crowd's hunger by having them "buy food for themselves." Jesus told them this was not the way.

Money is an abstraction, a concept. It is not Spirit. It is only a symbol, never the essence. The proper way to formulate a request is to ask directly for the essence of what is required. People who desire money usually are striving to attain feelings of security, peace of mind, freedom, and fun. If you ask for these *states of mind,* the universe will get you there in the most efficient way possible. The money will take care of itself.

4. Resist specifics. Note the wording of the request as it was formulated in the Alpha Passage. The disciples said the crowd needed "food." Jesus told the disciples to give them "something to eat."

No one asked for anything specific. No one asked for bread or for fish. The need was stated in very general terms. Being too specific greatly limits the universe and can cause serious delays in the manifestation process. Keeping things in general terms frees the universe to use the widest variety of means to deliver the essence of the dream and quickens the manifestation process significantly.

5. Honor the principle of integral need. First get into alignment. Become totally involved in the quest for Spirit, and for the attainment of compassion. When you do, certain needs will *naturally* arise. Now the universe will have a vested interest in keeping you abundantly supplied.

When you formulate a request to have a need filled that is an integral part of your true evolution, an integral part of Spirit's true evolution, the entire force of the universe will be behind you and miracles will occur easily and spontaneously.

6. Carefully avoid asking for things that will benefit only you. The request of a true miracle worker *always* includes others. *The more unselfish the request, the more power will be provided to enact your miracle.*

7. Although only you can decide what feelings you want to set up as goals, the following is excellent advice: Strongly consider including feelings of fun, happiness, relaxation, love, generosity, gratitude, and freedom in *all* of your requests.

Manifestation is a powerful process and requires great care. These seven key feelings will keep your miracle working safe, secure, and self-sustaining.

MAXIMIZING

Οἱ δὲ λέγουσιν αὐτῷ, Οὐκ ἔχομεν ὧδε εἰ μὴ πέντε ἄρτους
Oi de legousin auto Ouk echomen ode ei mi pente artous
But   say   to Him Not we have here except five   loaves

καὶ δύο ἰχθύας.   Ὁ δὲ εἶπε   Φέρετέ μοι αὐτοὺς ὧδε.
kai duo ichthuas.   O de eipe   Ferete moi autous ode.
and two fish.   He however said Bear to me them here.

I once knew a young doctor who was very unhappy with
his practice—and with his life. Although he was an excellent physician, his practice never seemed to prosper. Each
day he looked anxiously at the appointment book on his receptionist's desk hoping to see that it was filled with patients,
but each time he was disappointed. His expenses mounted
and he couldn't seem to make ends meet.

To make matters worse, he didn't like the area of the

country, the people in his neighborhood, or the weather in the region. He seemed completely out of place and was generally miserable. He experienced a low-grade depression nearly everyday. He lost hope and lost interest. Each day, he did the bare minimum on his cases, spending just enough time with each patient to get the job done. After work, he slouched home and spent the rest of the evening staring at the TV.

Then something happened to the young man. He started reading and thinking and listening in new ways and began to wonder: What would happen if he tried a completely new strategy?

He began to throw himself into his work, now doing as *much* as possible for every patient. Each time he walked into an exam room, he paid careful attention to everything that was going on, trying consciously to see the positive in every situation. If he had only a few appointments in the morning, he began looking at his free time as an opportunity. If he had only a few patients, he could spend just that much more time with them, asking them a lot of detailed questions about their health and their lives.

Steadily, things began to change. The patients loved the treatment they were getting. They asked the young doctor a lot of questions and received careful answers in an unhurried fashion. They began to bring their family members in and talked about him in glowing terms to their friends. Soon the friends began to see him and his appointment book was overflowing.

Then something miraculous happened. One year after starting his experiment, he got a spectacular job offer in a part of the country he had always loved. He handed his practice to another doctor, who was very happy with the location and clientele. After moving to his new practice, in an area far better suited to his personality and tastes, the quality of his life took a quantum leap upward.

The next section of the Alpha Passage shows us that the demonstrator did not create the loaves and fishes out of thin air. They did not appear from nothingness. Rather, the food which fed the crowd was an expansion of *existing* supply.

Imagine for a moment that you are in front of five thousand hungry people. Imagine that you ask everyone in the crowd to hand over any food that might exist, and you are presented with five loaves of bread and two fish.

What would *you* be thinking at this point?

This situation comes up in your life all the time, so it should be nothing new for you: You are lacking, you ask for help, and are presented with a seemingly pathetic and inadequate gift. How many times have you looked at that apparently small gift and fallen into a state of despair and frustration?

A miracle worker perceives things differently. A miracle worker always sees the supply that exists before him or her as a perfect beginning. The miracle worker always uses the supply in hand to the very maximum. If you learn to work with what you have, more will be given to you. This is one of the great laws. The universe watches you, and tests your attitudes and activities under various conditions. It is especially interested in the way you use what you have been given.

The parable of the talents relates the story of a man who goes away on a long trip and leaves his money to the care of his three servants. He gives the first servant five talents, the second servant two talents, and the third servant one talent. When he returns after a long absence, he asks the servants to show him what they have done with his money, how they have handled their test of stewardship. The first two servants tell the master they had faith in their charge. They kept the money in circulation, investing it wisely. They maximized the money's potential and, in doing so, doubled it.

Upon hearing this the master is very pleased and tells the two servants, "You have believed in a few things, I will make you master over many things." In essence, he tells them, "You passed the test. You have proven that you will use what I give you to the very limits of your ability. Therefore, you can obviously be trusted with more."

The last servant, by contrast, fails the test. He was only given a single talent to begin with. When the master asks him what he did with it, the servant says, "I was afraid, and I hid the talent in the earth." The servant acted out of fear. As a result, he saw only lack and failed to see the one talent's true potential. Hidden away in the earth, the talent failed to expand and multiply. The master, seeing that the servant is not a reliable steward, takes even the single talent away. He is left with nothing.

The world constantly monitors our actions to see how we use the resources we are given to oversee. If you are a good steward and consistently use what you have to the maximum, more and more will be diverted into the channels of your life. The universe is very careful. It hates waste. Those who use its precious energy with appropriate gratitude and care are invariably rewarded. Conversely, if you don't use your gifts, you can expect to lose them.

Basic universal laws apply: Form follows thought. Like attracts like. If you focus your attention on what you have, your consciousness will attract more. If you focus on what you lack, you will attract more lack. Positive or negative, whatever you emphasize in consciousness always expands.

You cannot circumvent this principle. It works with mathematical precision. If you focus on lack 98 percent of the time by worrying and fretting and then try to correct the situation with a few scattered, superficial affirmations, you will reap accordingly: Your life will still be 98 percent lacking.

Focus one-pointedly on what you have and *see* it as perfect. Use the resources you have at hand carefully, milking every possible bit of use from them. Do this cheerfully, gratefully, and as consistently as possible. When you can do this 10 percent of the time, you will find that your reality is 10 percent healed. When you can do this 100 percent of the time, you will have entered the dimension of the miraculous, you will have entered heaven.

Activating the Fourth Condition

1. Examine your problem carefully. Look at the request you have formulated. Before you ask for more, take an inventory of your existing supply in this area. Be extremely careful and thorough. Are you overlooking anything?

2. Ask yourself: Are you maximizing what you already have? If you are experiencing lack, you may well be tak-

ing what you have for granted, indulging in wistful envy about all the things you don't have.

3. Look through your things carefully. Look in your closets, your attic, your basement, and your garage. Look at all the things that have been entrusted to you that are lying dormant, completely taken for granted. See the supply that now exists.

Complacency could be a big part of the problem. Pay attention to all that you have been entrusted with. *Focus on what you have.* Make sure you are seeing everything you have with gratitude and using it to the maximum. It may take some time, but if you do this in good faith, Spirit will always give you more.

4. Look at your talents, your health, your knowledge, and your other *intangible* resources. These are every bit as important as your physical supply. Have you maximized the use of these profound gifts? If you haven't, correct the problem carefully and consciously.

GIVING

Οἱ δὲ λέγουσιν αὐτῷ, Οὐκ ἔχομεν ὧδε εἰ μὴ πέντε ἄρτους
Oi de legousin auto Ouk echomen ode   ei mi pente artous
But   say   to Him Not we have here except   five   loaves

καὶ δύο ἰχθύας.   Ὁ δὲ εἶπε   Φέρετέ μοι αὐτοὺς ὧδε.
kai duo ichthuas.   O de eipe   Ferete moi autous ode.
and two   fish.   He however said Bear to me them here.

Juárez, Mexico: A priest serving the area becomes con-
cerned about a situation developing at a massive garbage
dump on the edge of the city. Many poverty-stricken individuals actually live in the filthy dump, scavenging food and
other supplies to stay alive. The priest decides to deliver dinner to these people one day. He plans to feed about one hundred and twenty-five people and prepares food sufficient for
that number.

To the dismay of the priest, however, four hundred hungry people turn out for the event. But he does his best to maintain an attitude of faith and trust. As he watches in amazement, everyone in the crowd appears to have plenty to eat. When everyone has had their fill, he hands out large bags of leftovers. After dropping their food at home, some of the people even return and fill their bags a second time.

When the feast is over and everyone goes home, excess food *still* remains. It is gathered up and taken to an orphanage. The orphanage uses the food for a big dinner. Once again leftovers remain. They are gathered and given to a second orphanage. As the gift of food is released and freely passed along, it multiplies in a miraculous way.

The Miracle of the Loaves and Fishes occurs in the same way. The flow begins with a sincere gift. According to the account given in the gospel of John, a small boy is the source of the original bread and fish. Presumably he is as hungry as everyone else but generously offers what little he has to the disciples. With the innocence and trust of a child, he releases his precious resources, freely and in good faith, to the higher good.

The disciples pass the food forward to Jesus, who keeps things moving by raising the gift above his head—in essence giving the gift to the Source. The chain of giving continues as the food is then given back to the disciples, who in turn distribute it to the crowd. Each time the bread is passed along, its potential increases and it further expands.

The Fifth Condition is closely related to the First Condition—establishing emptiness. The act of giving relieves congestion and stimulates the flow and increase of resources.

Activating the Fifth Condition

1. *Focus on the feeling behind the gift.* To be sure, the physical release of the gift has power and is an essential part of the Fifth Condition. But the *intent* behind the gift is the real power. As always, the conditions of a miracle work primarily at the level of consciousness. The generosity and love motivating you to give are the ultimate stimuli for the flow that results.

Like attracts like. The feelings of satisfaction and joy that result from true giving attract objects and experiences that will promote more feelings of satisfaction and joy in your life. There is a simple test you can use to evaluate any gift: You will know that a gift is capable of generating miraculous results if the act of giving that gift makes you feel really good. It's very simple. You should never "give until it hurts." If the act of giving causes you worry or discomfort, your pain will attract more pain. Giving should *always* feel good.

2. Whenever possible, remain anonymous. Generosity is a form of compassion. When you give in a generous manner, you are being *moved with* compassion. Putting your feelings of generosity into *action* aligns you solidly with the current and puts the full flow of the universe behind you. True generosity seeks no return and no acknowledgment. Generosity must be selfless if it is to work miracles. Staying anonymous helps you stay selfless. When you give anonymously, you keep your ego on the sideline and stay true to the mark.

3. Take care to attach no strings of any kind. A true gift is always released freely. If a gift is given with any expectation that the recipient will act or think in any specific way as a result, the gift will be ineffective in promoting your own miracle. Never give to manipulate someone in any way, however subtle. When you give, let go completely.

4. Avoid codependent giving. Certain gifts can actually cause harm. For example, tourists visiting the mountains like to feed the marmots and chipmunks in the summer. But these gifts of food rob them of the ability

to forage and fend for themselves in the winter when the tourists are gone. Many animals perish as a result.

Favor charities which teach people to help themselves. In general, avoid giving money to those who have chronic problems providing for themselves. This will only weaken them. Sometimes, it is better to give your time and attention instead.

5. Expect your return to come from the right place. When you begin true giving, the universe may test you. Sometimes the recipients of your charity will show little or no gratitude—especially when you give anonymously. Don't think twice about this. The more you expect gratitude from humans, the *less* will result.

The kind of giving that facilitates miracles involves a major shift in your consciousness. Completely forget about the reactions of the human beings who receive your gifts. Expect your true return—*all of it*—from the universe itself. Form follows thought. When you expect the return from people, people can be the only channel for your return. When you expect your return from the universe, you open the universe as a channel for your return. Which channel would you really prefer?

6. Don't neglect your microenvironment. Charity be-

gins at home. A very common pitfall is to give generously to high-profile charities while ignoring the immediate environment. First things first. Correct any
deficiency in your relationship with your spouse, your
children, your parents, and your coworkers. Gifts of
time, attention, understanding, cooperation, and acceptance are some of the most powerful gifts you can
ever give.

Remember to stay selfless and low profile. Keep
your intentions to yourself. Don't let anyone know
what you are doing. Give freely. Expect no return whatever, even from those close to you.

7. Give consciously and thoughtfully. When you give
money to charities, do so carefully. *Think* about what
you are doing. Take time to study the charities and pro-
grams available to you. It is important to know if a charity is efficient or if it wastes money. Does it help people
help themselves? It is your responsibility under universal law to know the answers to these kinds of questions.

If you are careful and conscientious in your giving, the universe will be careful and conscientious with
your gifts. Giving in a mechanical, automatic manner is
useless.

8. Don't limit your gifts to money. This is a huge mistake. Expand your concept of gifts. Whenever possible, give your personal essence and spirit. Your time and attention are especially powerful gifts. Give them freely and consistently. Don't try to substitute money for your spirit.

9. Give the gift of listening. It can be one of the finest of all gifts. Listening is a gift of consciousness. It is a terrific way to give your time and attention. Ask your family, coworkers, and friends about themselves. Then be quiet and listen. Keep asking questions. Take your time and don't hurry. Be generous and sincerely interested. Talking about yourself can be a good way of sharing. But more often than not, talking is a way of taking—it takes up other people's time and attention. Learn to shift your emphasis to listening.

Miraculous and serendipitous things can be learned in this way. When you become a listener, people start telling you things. The universe often delivers precious bits of information in this way. Listen and prosper.

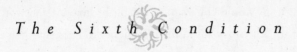

GROUNDING

Καὶ κελεύσας τούς ὄχλους ἀνακλιθῆναι ἐπὶ τούς χόρτους,

Kai kelefsas tous ochlous anaklithinai epi tou chortous,

And commanding the crowds to recline on the grass,

What if you wanted a great deal of energy to flow through you? What could you do to make sure the power flowed very freely and abundantly through your life? Obviously, we are not talking about physical power necessarily but rather *meta*physical power—the kind of power that enables the miraculous. However, much can be learned about the way metaphysical power flows by studying the way physical power flows, for both are governed by similar laws and behave in much the same way.

Take electrical power for example. If you wanted a great deal of electricity to flow through your body, what kinds of conditions would you want to establish? Imagine that you are beneath a light socket in the basement. You are standing on a wooden stool and wearing thick rubber boots. Now, you put your finger in the light socket. What happens?

If the boots are thick enough, nothing happens. No current flows through your body. The wood of the stool and the rubber in the boots insulate you completely from the ground. So, when you stick your finger in the socket, the electricity has no where to go, no where to flow.

Now imagine that you take the boots off and stand in your bare feet on the damp concrete of the basement floor. What happens if you stick your finger in the light socket this time? Obviously, a powerful surge of electricity passes through you. This time you are *grounded,* i.e., your body is in firm contact with the ground. Now the electrical current has somewhere to go.

The earth provides a perfect destination for the charged particles coming from the light socket because it has a very "neutral charge," which is just another way of saying that it has an extremely low concentration of charged particles. Because the earth is relatively "empty" of charged electrons, it functions as a kind of vacuum. And you already know from the First Condition how a vacuum automatically "pulls" flow toward it. When a path such as a wire connects a concentrated charge of electrons to the earth, the electrons rush through the wire into this vacuum in an attempt to fill it. This is how a flow of electricity is created.

The energy that supplies the power for miracles moves in much the same way as electrical energy. Jesus fed large numbers of people by expanding small amounts of food on two different occasions. What's interesting is that on *both* occasions he told everyone present to "sit down on the grass" just before the proliferation occurred. There was a reason for this. The miracle worker knew that the requisite degree of energy could only flow out of him and through the hungry people if they were properly grounded.

Throughout nature, flow goes to the lowest point. Water flows to the lowest point in a watershed or a system of pipes. That's why water could once again begin to flow into the anxious farmer's pond. Once he had drained the stagnant water away, low-lying areas were left that could accept the flow of new water. Air masses flow from areas of high pressure to areas of low pressure—a process that produces the winds in our atmosphere. Heat flows from areas of high temperature to areas of low temperature.

The same principle explains the processes of flow that are observed in other kinds of systems. For example, in economic systems, commodities flow from areas of excess to areas of shortage, via a rule called the law of supply and demand. Knowledge flows from people who know to people who need to know. Grounding is the act of connecting a high point to a low point so that a process of flow can take place. Grounding can be used to increase the flow of any kind of energy and is a vital part of the miracle worker's tool kit.

Matthew 9:20 relates a classic story which illustrates how the principle of grounding works in a practical sense. The Nazarene was walking through a crowd when he suddenly felt a huge amount of energy being pulled from his body. He stopped and turned. A woman who had been hemorrhaging for twelve years had stolen up behind him and touched the hem of his robe. As she did, a great current of energy was discharged into her body, and she was instantly healed.

The important point of the story is that this woman *pulled* the energy from Jesus. The wording of the story makes it clear that he did not consciously direct it toward her. He didn't even know she was there. She had grounded herself so perfectly that she was able to pull a powerful current of healing energy into herself. She had accomplished this at the level of Spirit. Her faith had grounded her. Her belief had opened her to receive the flow.

And so it is with the power you will receive from the universe as your miracle unfolds. It is a mistake to expect that the universe will direct its energy toward you automatically. It is up to *you* to position yourself so that you can pull the energy you need from the Source. How is this done? You will ground yourself at the level of Spirit by waking up in the present moment, by seeing a positive outcome, and by trusting. The power of the current that flows through you will be directly proportional to the strength of your conviction.

Careful translation reveals another dimension to this passage. The Greek words for "sit down on the grass" are *"anaklithinai epi tou chortou." Anaklithinai* means to recline or lie back. Although *chortou* can be translated as "grass or vegetation," it also can be used to refer more generally to "a garden."

This is a very odd thing to say to people who are in the middle of the desert. Telling people to lie back in the garden doesn't really make sense from a literal standpoint. There is no grass in a desert and certainly no garden. Therefore, this unusual phrase must have a deeper, metaphorical level of meaning. It turns out that this deeper level isn't difficult to uncover.

The use of the word "garden" is very reminiscent of the Garden of Eden. Indeed, exploring this metaphor yields a wealth of pertinent metaphysical information which is completely consistent with the conditions of a miracle. Consider: The story of the Garden of Eden is a metaphor for the development of human consciousness. The original, natural state of human beings is like that of a child. A child has not yet "eaten of the tree of knowledge."

As a result, a child is wholly in the present moment without the burden of self-consciousness, judgment, and self-doubt. She is free to experience things just as they are. She does not judge. She feels no shame or "nakedness." Being just as she is in the garden of the present, a child is perfectly grounded to receive the flow. As a result, she experiences no lack and has everything she needs in great abundance.

This is why Jesus said that we must become as children if we are to enter the kingdom of heaven. We have to be able to think and act and feel like a child if we are to return to the paradise we have lost. To "lay back in the garden" is to relax and return to a natural childlike state of mind.

By meditating and by dwelling in the present, you will perceive things differently. This shift in perception plays a critical role in the enactment of miracles. When your consciousness is altered in this way, the doors of perception will open and you will be able to *see* the beauty and abundance that exists in great profusion all around you. And through this process of grounding you will put yourself in a position to receive your abundance.

Did Jesus mean to convey all of this when he told the crowd to "lie back in the garden" or was he only speaking in a literal sense? That depends on how smart and how deep you think he really was.

Activating the Sixth Condition

1. Stay in the present moment as much as possible. The past and future do not exist. They are constructs of the imagination. Since the present is the only real place you can be, it is the only place that you can *receive* anything of real value. Only when you are firmly grounded in the here and now will you be positioned to accept the flow. In addition, the present is the only place that you can act. It is the only solid platform from which you can *do* real things to advance your dream.

Fear and anxiety, which form the great dam that blocks your flow, are a byproduct of an obsession with the future. Shame and guilt result from thinking about the past and obsessing over the self. When you are fully grounded in the present—just "being"—these obstacles dissolve like mist in the sun, and the energy of your life begins to flow with great power. As you go through your day, return to the present over and over again. Wake up and prosper.

2. Become as a child. You will return to the garden by returning to your natural state of consciousness. *Learn to play again.* Make time to do things that are fun, things that make you laugh, things that bring you joy. In the end, you will see that this was an enormous part of your abundance, your miracle. It is incredibly easy and yet so hard for us adults.

Don't waste all of your time anxiously slaving away at one arduous task after another. This is an enormous mistake. Take your life into your hands and start living. Do the things you have always wanted to do. Start *now.* Now is the only time that exists.

3. Spend time with children. Children know more about pure being than you. Learn from them. I can promise you, if you can't get down on the floor and play with a child, you will never be able to work miracles. *Loosen up, lighten up, and prosper.*

4. Ground out physically. Take your shoes off! Wade in a stream. Walk on the lawn. Get outside and get in contact. Lighten up! Slow down and smell the roses: The garden is all around you.

5. Work on your level of belief. Become as the woman in the crowd. Know that the power will flow to you, *even if you but lightly touch the Spirit in consciousness.* Never accept failure in this area.

If you don't believe, *make* yourself believe. If you can't make yourself believe, then *fake* it! Act and talk like you really do believe. If you feel foolish doing this, remind yourself that the alternative is clearly a dead end. You've been down that path and know perfectly well where it leads. Now you need to try the path of belief. What have you got to lose?

Over and over, reprogram your mind at the deepest possible level to believe and receive. It may take time. You may repeatedly fall as you practice this critical skill. Like every seeker and every saint, you will struggle with terrible doubts and tests of your faith. But, like a child learning to ride a bicycle, you will eventually succeed and live to see your miracle unfold.

VISUALIZING

καὶ λαβὼν τοὺς πέντε ἄρτους καὶ τοὺς δύο ἰχθύας,

kai lavon tous pente artous kai tous duo ichthuas,

and taking the five loaves and the two fishes,

ἀναβλέψας εἰς τὸν οὐρανὸν,

anavlepsas eis ton ouranon,

looking up to the Heaven,

One August afternoon several years ago, while writing on my laptop in the call room, I heard over the hospital intercom the ominous words, "Dr. Michael to ER stat." Contrary to popular belief, the word "stat" is rarely used except on television and invariably signals an especially desperate situation.

As I rushed into the emergency room, I saw one of my most beloved patients lying helplessly on the gurney, nurses swirling anxiously around her. Her color was horrible, and she was gasping for breath. She was barely conscious. One glance at her EKG told me she had sustained a massive myocardial infarction.

This woman was a good friend as well as a good patient. She was the wife of one of the local ministers and a valued person in the community. She had a loving family and a devoted husband. I wanted very much for her to survive and began working in earnest to stabilize her rapidly deteriorating condition. This one was personal. High flow oxygen and wide bore IVs were started. Nitroglycerine, aspirin, and other medications were given. I quickly initiated steps to administer a powerful drug that could dissolve the blood clot that had formed in one of her coronary arteries.

But as I watched the monitor at her bedside, it rapidly became apparent that she was dying. The clot-dissolving drug wouldn't be started in time. As I surveyed the situation, my senses received a barrage of ominous information. The monitor showed that her blood pressure was plummeting and her pulse falling into the forties. With my eyes, I saw her losing consciousness and the dusky tint of her skin deepening. I watched as potentially lethal rhythms began to dance on the heart monitor, even though appropriate medications were given to counteract them. I prepared to put a tube in to help her breathe.

I began to take inventory. I had done everything humanly possible, at least from a medical standpoint. I had no other measures available at my command. In spite of my best efforts, she was clearly going to die. The damage to her heart muscle was too extensive. By my estimate she had only a few minutes left before the final lethal arrhythmias set in.

When I was fifteen, my father died suddenly in front of me from a massive heart attack, and I began to have fleeting flashbacks of that fateful day. I lapsed into a desolate depression, preparing myself grimly for my patient's ultimate demise. How could I tell her family? How would they go on? All of this took place in the space of a few brief minutes.

And then something occurred to me: I had not yet applied the conditions of a miracle. God knows we needed one, and we needed one right now. I had been studying the conditions of miracles. What on earth was the matter with me? The moment was at hand; I had to at least try.

I was already moved with compassion, that wasn't a problem. Any decent person would have felt compassion for this woman. But I added to this by quickly emptying my mind of all thoughts and then formulating a simple request in general terms: "I ask that this woman be healed."

I waited. Still nothing happened. In the next two minutes, she continued to worsen dramatically. She only had another minute or two. Then I realized—how could I have been so dense? I had failed to *see the desired end*. I had failed to pray for her *believing*, seeing in my mind's eye that she was lying free of pain and discomfort, and that her EKG had normalized.

But how could I do this? It was absurd. How was I supposed to see this in my mind's eye when I *knew* as a doctor, as a scientist, that all of her physiological parameters clearly indicated a swift and certain death? Although I was seeing disaster with my physical eyes, I would have to see something better with the eyes of Spirit. I would have to elevate my vision to a higher state.

This, I have come to know, is the real challenge. This is one of the main reasons we are here on this earth. An important part of our whole purpose as human beings is to *learn how to see the best, even as the worst transpires in livid detail before our very eyes.* That is one of our greatest and most important tasks as humans.

I had hit bottom. What did I have to lose?

It was a very good question.

In spite of my well-founded doubts, I quickly formed a picture of her lying peacefully on the table, talking to me normally as she always had. Although I felt a bit foolish as I did this, I forced myself to do it anyway.

The mental image of this person healed and happy contrasted so sharply with what I was seeing physically that it took every ounce of conviction to continue. At the same time, I focused on the great source of all true power, remembering grimly that I had absolutely no power over the situation. *I* could not heal her. *I* could not perform a miracle. *I* could do nothing effective. But Spirit could do anything, even that which was impossible. And I had asked nothing for myself. If this woman would be healed, the entire community would be benefited. I let go and put the situation in the hands of the Infinite and instantly felt more relaxed. It wasn't my problem anymore. Whatever happened now was up to God.

I remember the next thing I did was to walk around the table. She was having a problem with one of her IV lines, and I wanted to make some minor adjustments. When I reached the other side of the table and touched her arm, she opened her eyes, looked straight at me and said, "I'm OK, doctor. How are you doing today? I'm so glad to see you." One glance at the monitor told me her blood pressure and pulse were now in a safe range.

Although I managed to preserve my professional demeanor, I was nearly paralyzed. This was entirely impossible. In the space of sixty seconds she had gone from a state of "extremis," or imminent death, to a state of near normalcy. Even the most dramatic response to the medications I had given her couldn't come close to explaining this nearly instantaneous transformation.

There was no mistake. Her blood pressure had turned around, her skin had pinked up nicely, and her level of consciousness was virtually normal. Her chest pain was gone and the malignant arrhythmias I had been watching nervously on the monitor had resolved. She was breathing easily, and the pulse oxymeter blinking above the bed indicated a normal level of oxygenation. As I rode with her in the ambulance to the cardiac cath lab for definitive treatment, she remained in good condition and went on to live many more years.

Did the process of visualization really help save her or was this just a coincidence? I will never know for sure. But I do know that all of my acquaintances and colleagues that have attempted similar visualization processes have had similar, surprising results. For example, as I taught a course on the Twelve Conditions one Sunday afternoon, a petite, well-dressed woman in the back row of the sanctuary raised her hand as we discussed this very point. She explained that she was a neurosurgeon who had superspecialized in problems with the blood vessels of the brain. During a particularly harrowing operation on a woman patient, a set of complex and unavoidable circumstances caused the patient to have a massive stroke. The entire right side of her body was totally and irreversibly paralyzed.

The surgeon, a particularly compassionate and sensitive individual, was badly shaken. As the unfortunate woman lay in the ICU on a ventilator, she agonized over the situation, wondering how she would tell the patient what had happened when she regained consciousness. The situation was hopeless, a tragedy of the worst sort.

She went on to tell the class that she had read about the seventh condition of a miracle and wondered if it might be helpful. Like me, she thought to herself, "What can it hurt? What have I got to lose?" In her mind's eye, she began seeing the patient sitting up, waving her right hand and smiling. Although she saw no immediate change, her faith, like her character, was strong and she persisted.

Three days later she walked into the patient's room and saw something totally shocking, something amazing and wonderful: The patient was sitting up in bed, waving her right hand and smiling broadly.

. . .

Although the traditional translation of the passage from Matthew states that Jesus "looked up to heaven," an entirely different dimension of meaning for this passage is disclosed by careful translation.

The act of "looking up to heaven" is described by two interesting Greek words. The first is *anavlepsas*. This word can mean simply "to look" as traditional translations indicate but it also means to "restore vision."

The second word is *ouranon*. It is true that this can be translated simply as "heaven," but there are other shades of meaning. According to *Strong's Exhaustive Concordance, ouranon* also means "power" or "happiness." Key to the definition of this word is the idea of "elevation."

"Looking up to heaven" is a way of focusing attention on the Source. Consistently remembering where all resources originate empowers a miracle worker—and leads to the realm of happiness.

Form follows thought. The channel or pipeline that will connect you with the Source is not made of tile or plastic, it is made of consciousness. When your thoughts focus on the Source and dwell at the Source, you will establish contact with the Source. Then, if you are properly grounded . . .

There is only one Source for all forms of supply. This Source unfortunately has many names, which fosters the nonsensical notion that there are many different sources. The Source is known variously as God, the Creator, the Provider, Providence, Grace, the One, the Universe, the Universal Mind, Infinite Intelligence, the Collective Unconscious, Yahweh, Allah, Brahma, the Atman, the Universal Field, the Great Spirit, Nature, the Light, the Oversoul—the list goes on and on. In spite of this apparent diversity, which is nothing more than an artifact of human language, all of these refer to the same thing.

Because there is only one Source, and because everything in the universe comes from this Source, every individual kind of matter and energy is, in reality, a different form or manifestation of the same *substance* as it originates at the fountainhead. And what exactly is this primordial substance? As many quantum physicists have begun to suspect, it is not a subatomic particle like a lepton or a quark: It is *consciousness*.

Regardless of its form, every single thing in the universe is alive and conscious—in spite of the fact that our very limited intelligence and senses might have us believe otherwise. Every type of matter and energy in your reality is a form of consciousness, a manifestation of consciousness. This is why you have to reshape your consciousness in order to reshape your reality. This is why you have to make a conscious decision in order to enter the dimension of the miraculous.

As a species, we human beings are very visually oriented. A huge portion of our brain is involved in one way or another with visual images. This is why, when we change what happens in the mind's eye, we change how we think and feel at an extraordinarily deep level.

Nearly everyone is familiar with the mental technique known as visualization. In visualization, a clear mental picture of a desired end is consciously cultivated. This is a tremendously efficient way of reshaping consciousness. Although there is some degree of variation in the specific techniques recommended, virtually every authority on self-help and self-empowerment recognizes the immense importance of visualization. Positive visualization clearly lifts the consciousness from thoughts of lack and failure into a higher realm of power and happiness.

Because form follows thought, forms within your reality will shift to manifest what you are visualizing and circumstances will improve as your consciousness shifts to a higher level. All miracle workers use this principle, although they may describe and explain it differently. This is the true meaning of the phrase "looking up to heaven." Matthew 21:22 alludes to this principle: *"And all things, whatsoever you shall ask in prayer, believing, you shall receive."* We often say that we will believe something when we see it. Seeing *is* believing.

When you see yourself, in your mind's eye, complete with everything you need, you will *believe* that state has already come to pass. Then, since form always follows thought and because like attracts like, what you believe will automatically manifest in solid form in your reality.

Matthew's passage tells us something important about the demonstrator's internal thought processes at this critical point in the miracle. It indicates that he was *seeing* in his mind's eye that the crowd was adequately supplied. He *must* have had this mental image. His subsequent actions clearly reflect this, because the next thing he did was to begin feeding the crowd—confidently, generously, and without the slightest hesitation. He couldn't have proceeded in this way without having a clear picture of the final state.

The third condition of a miracle is established by formulating a request and placing it into words. The seventh condition is established by "restoring the vision"—*by seeing anew the successful fulfillment of this request in the mind's eye as if it was real in the here and now.* When the final visualization burns steadily in the mind's eye without flickering, the miracle quickly manifests in response.

The promptness of the response is proportional to the

depth and clarity of the vision. Achieving this degree of faith and clarity is challenging but within the reach of every human being. It takes time and practice, but everyone, without exception, is capable of this shift in awareness.

The proper way to visualize is to see the end state in the mind's eye while simultaneously focusing on the Source. "Look up to heaven" *at the same time* that you restore your vision to its naturally elevated state. This keeps the self out of the process. As long as you are focused on the Source, the ego is in the backseat where it belongs. "You" are not manifesting the desired circumstances. You have no power to do so. Only Spirit has sufficient energy to get the job done.

People make a huge mistake in believing they are responsible for the changes they experience in their personal realities when they engage in miracle work. In actuality, your mind commands a very small amount of power. The true power behind a miracle comes from the Source. The visualization only provides *direction* for the power. It is like a wire that connects a source of electrical energy to an appliance. The act of *seeing the final state* opens the mind so that it can function as a directed channel.

Action Steps for the Seventh Condition

1. Always begin by reviewing the work you did with the third condition. Remember clearly what you are really striving for. Remember the *essence* of your needs. Design your visualization very carefully based on the request you have formulated.

2. Don't be unduly specific. Don't see "things" manifesting. See yourself *having the feelings and experiences* that form the basis of your request. Keeping things in general terms will leave as many options, as many avenues as possible open to the universe to fill the order.

Don't see a specific house. See yourself living comfortably, feeling secure and deeply satisfied. Don't see a specific man or woman that you want to be your soul mate. See your self in a great relationship feeling happy and fulfilled. Don't see your bank account swelling with money. See yourself free of worry, generously supplied, and secure. Like attracts like. The quality of your thoughts will attract the appropriate circumstances automatically.

3. *See the desired end as if it had already occurred.* No matter how impossible your request, see your miracle com-

plete and whole in your mind's eye. Demand to see. Dare to see.

4. Feel the *feelings* you will feel in your heaven. You are not a mind alone. The body can "visualize," too, a process called *somatic visualization*. You have a body with many centers of energy. When these centers feel what they will feel when the dream merges with reality, they are visualizing. Sometimes somatic visualization produces the fastest and most dramatic results of all. The addition of details engaging the senses of smell, taste, touch, and hearing engages some of the deepest and most ancient parts of the brain and greatly enhances the visualization process.

5. Know exactly how to handle doubts that arise during the visualization process. Whenever you experience any doubt, immediately see the doubt for what it is. Don't try to fight it or suppress it. And don't waste one iota of energy *fretting* about the fact that you're having the doubt. Doubts are normal and mean nothing.

If you have a doubt, just look at it dispassionately, matter-of-factly, as if to say, "Oh, that's interesting. A doubt is running through my mind. *I'll just calmly turn that over to Infinite Intelligence to be quietly deactivated.* That way, only my positive thoughts and feelings will generate effects in my reality."

The great news is that once you become conscious of a doubt and turn it over to Spirit, *it immediately ceases to generate effects within your reality, even though it may continue to run through your mind.* This is the only effective strategy for handling a doubt. Never, under any circumstances, deny a doubt or attempt to struggle with it. This only funnels more energy into it and increases its power to generate negative effects within your personal reality.

6. Don't forget to stay focused on the higher good. *Don't get off track with visualizations that benefit only you.* This will take you out of alignment with the great current that can speed you to your goal. Don't miss the mark. Your final goal is a state of perfect love and compassion. *Always think of others first during your miracle work.*

The Eighth Condition

GRATITUDE

εὐλόγησε

evlogise

He blessed

The Greek word used here is *evlogise*. A modern derivative is the word "eulogy." *Evlogise* can indeed mean "to bless." But it also means, more generally, "to praise, speak well of, or give thanks for."

Evlogise is a particularly interesting word. The first portion, *ev,* means good. The second portion, *logise,* comes from the Greek *logos* which, as we discussed in the introduction, is arguably the deepest term in the entire Greek language.

In its most superficial sense, *logos* simply means "word." Although standard biblical translations rarely go any deeper, it is important to understand that *logos* refers to much more than a written or spoken word. *Logos* also refers to the thought or idea that is the source of the word.

Words have extraordinary power. Because they express thoughts, words are forces that have the ability to change and create. Thoughts and ideas are the impulses that make things happen in this world. Every human accomplishment, great and small, can be traced back to a thought. Every enterprise, invention, and work of art—and every miracle—begins as an idea. Words are the agents that channel the force of miraculous ideas out of the mind and into the world.

Knowing this gives us important insight into the true nature of the demonstrator's "blessing." In essence, the blessing of the bread was a careful continuation of the seventh condition: Jesus elevated his vision, seeing the crowd happy and well fed. He then brought the positive thought form to a more concrete level by putting his thoughts into words. As everyone listened, he spoke highly of the bread. The essence of his blessing was this: "This supply is perfect, it is abundant in quantity, exquisite in quality, and very generously supplied. How grateful we are to receive such a gift."

In contemporary terms, this eulogy, this blessing would be called an *affirmation*. Affirmations channel the power of positive thought forms from the confines of the mind into the world, where they can set real changes into motion. It all comes back to the great law: Like attracts like. When you focus on the good, letting your thoughts dwell on all the great things in your life, you attract even greater good. When you lift your thoughts to a higher level of solidity by putting them into words and verbally affirming your good, you greatly facilitate the process. *The mindset that underlies this process is called gratitude.*

Miracle workers are invariably filled with gratitude. They eat, sleep, and breathe gratitude. There is not a whiner or complainer among them. Miracle workers always experience every event, every moment with profound appreciation. They find great delight in the simple gifts that life offers and never waste time wishing for more. They constantly verbalize their positivity as approval and support and are endlessly giving thanks. They invariably speak well of others. The grateful are very close to God as well. As Noela Evans once said, "Gratitude is the language of the angels." Quite naturally, the universe smiles upon such individuals and showers them with great abundance.

Here's a little exercise to show you why this is so. Think about a gift you gave that was greatly appreciated, a gift that was used to the maximum by the recipient. Now think about a gift you gave that was taken for granted and thus wasted. Consider the two people who received these gifts. To which person did you want to give more? Why should you expect the universe to feel any differently about its gifts to you? Divine intelligence generally won't go too far out of its way to provide for you in a miraculous way if you are negative and complacent about the gifts you have already received.

Activating the Eighth Condition

1. Bless your resources. *All of them. All the time.* Be acutely conscious of the gifts you have received. Cultivate a sense of appreciation at a deep level and express your feelings of gratitude in words.

Begin now to make frequent, positive comments about your health, your friends, your job, your house, your country, your life, and everything else you have been given. Don't wait for things to be grateful for. *Actively search* for things to be grateful for. Be thankful for what you have. Never insult the Giver.

2. While staying grounded in the moment, shift your mindset from one of jaded complacency and boredom to one of childlike wonder and amazement. Work at this carefully. When your perception shifts, your reality will shift.

The shift to wonderment is the door that opens into the higher dimension. This alone, when executed perfectly, will enable you to pass into a new world in which dreams and reality merge effortlessly and naturally in a river of lavish abundance.

3. Verbalize the fulfillment of your dream. See your dream as reality and frequently put your vision into written and spoken words. *Speak well* of your dream, your heaven. Never speak any words that support a reality different from the one you seek to create.

4. Never let a negative word pass your lips. This can be difficult at first but is well within your reach. In a way, we like to complain. It gives us a kind of perverse pleasure. We complain to fit in, to impress others, and to elicit sympathy. But these are dubious goals at best.

Begin now to follow the old adage, "If you can't say something nice, don't say anything at all." When others complain, restrain yourself. Don't jump in. Don't let others drag you down to their level. Keep your thoughts and words positive. Others will admire you for doing so. Thinking in a pessimistic and hypercritical manner is bad enough—don't make matters worse by giving your negative thoughts the power to manifest by putting them into words. Hold your tongue. Never speak ill of another. Never gossip.

Concentrate on improving your own state of mind and let the world take care of itself. Follow this rule of thumb: When things are good, say good things. When things are bad, say twice as many good things.

ACTING AS IF

καὶ κλάσας

kai klasas

and broke

ry to put yourself in the demonstrator's place at this point in the miracle. Imagine what he would feel like: Five thousand famished people—perhaps seven thousand counting the women and children—are all watching with great intensity. Imagine the kind of pressure you would feel. You have given indications that you are going to do something that will defy all the known laws of time and space—that you are going to feed the entire crowd. And yet you only have a single armload of food. You offer your blessing and . . . now what? What are you going to do?

Without missing a beat, Jesus simply starts breaking the bread. In other words, he began to *act,* and acted *as if* the existing supply were sufficient to meet the needs of the crowd. Without hesitation and with perfect confidence, he began to break the existing food into smaller and smaller fragments. He completed this stage of decisive action by distributing the fragments to the crowd.

The most important thing to remember about acting "as if" is that it begins with *acting.* Miracle workers don't just say prayers and visualize. They act. They *do* things. They break through the barriers of inertia and doubt and get moving. Miracle workers know that if they do not act, no one else will. And they also know that when they act, they have to act with perfect confidence.

The idle never prosper. Spirit helps those that help themselves. The universe funnels its energy into the lives of those who act, those who work, those who make an effort to actually get things accomplished. Prayer, visualization, and affirmation are wonderful things. But alone they are insufficient to produce results. At some point you have to set your thoughts and dreams in motion if you are to see them materialize. Don't just sit there. To arrive at the desired destination, you will have to move. Transforming your current reality to the reality of your dreams is a dynamic process. Action will be required to mobilize the necessary series of changes.

An idea is the first level of the manifestation process. Visualization is the second level. Somatic visualization—*feeling* the appropriate feelings in the body as if they were already real—is the third level. Putting your ideas and visualizations into spoken words *as if* they were already real is the fourth level, and putting things into written words is the fifth.

The sixth level of creation involves *acting as if* the intended creation is real—as if it is happening *right now*. This step offers the most daunting leap of faith of all the steps. Part of you will worry that you will fall flat on your face, that you will make a fool of yourself. That is how leaps of faith are. But you will have to leap anyway if you ever expect to make any progress.

WHAT TO EXPECT

After you have prepared the ground by carefully establishing the previous conditions and have then begun to act, you can expect manifestation to begin. Just remember the role of time.

A true master can bring about manifestation in an instant. A master has attained perfect stillness of the mind and is perfectly grounded in the present. A master is perfectly compassionate and perfectly aligned with the great flow of energy. A master is perfectly giving and has perfect conviction behind his visualizations and affirmations. A master acts confidently and without hesitation. A master's manifestation occurs very rapidly.

But beginners do not possess such perfection. As a result, they can expect the process of manifestation to take some time. Expect a delay. Don't let it surprise you or discourage you. If you plant a seed, it will appear as though nothing is happening during the germination period. But beneath the surface where you cannot see, myriad complex processes are unfolding with mathematical precision, processes which must be established before the first shoots become visible. Be patient. Trust. Resist the temptation to dig up the seed to see what it is doing, or you may do irreparable harm.

It is important for the beginner to understand the delays that are an organic part of the miracle working process. The new miracle worker should never be surprised or upset by delay. The delay process should always be accepted gracefully. If not, there will be much unnecessary discouragement: You may end up perceiving failure when, in reality, steady growth is proceeding normally.

Activating the Ninth Condition

1. Stop dreaming and visualizing and start *doing*. Mental efforts will never succeed alone. Begin *now*. There is never any other time to begin. The ability to initiate action is absolutely critical. Procrastination has poisoned many a great dream.

2. As you start to act, refuse to let any delay surprise or discourage you. You are still learning about miracles. It is silly to expect the instantaneous results of a master miracle worker. Expect a miracle, but expect it to unfold in its own time. Although it can be hard, especially when you are in pain, you must exercise patience.

People always ask, "How long will my dream take?" The answer is that it will take as long as it will take. Your dream is a living thing. It has to grow organically, at its own rate.

Dreams are very much like trees. Large trees take longer to grow than small trees. If you intend to manifest something large and complex, fully expect it to take more time than something smaller and simpler. But know this: The more *accepting* you are about the time frame, the *shorter* it will be. It's an interesting paradox of

miracle work: Acceptance, patience, and a trusting attitude always keep the time involved to a minimum.

3. *Persist*. No matter what happens, keep acting, keep
going. One of the most effective catch phrases you can
use to establish the twelve conditions is "Keep going."
No matter where in the process you get stuck, apply this
motto as an automatic part of the solution. Keep your
sights set on the goal and keep moving toward it. Success has always belonged to the persistent. Persistence
can compensate for many other shortcomings.

4. Learn how to deal with snags, stumbling blocks, and
mental inertia. If you are stymied by a task or problem
that is particularly large or daunting, tackle the job with
this two step technique:

First, break the job down into several smaller steps.
Make these steps as simple as possible and figure out
which is the very first. Second, determine a time of the
week or time of the day when you are at *your very highest
energy*. Carefully set that time aside for one purpose and
one purpose only: to execute the first of the small steps
that will break the stumbling block. Schedule this time in
writing.

This is critical. Under no circumstances should you
attempt to accomplish something difficult when you

are at a low energy ebb. You are only setting yourself up for failure and frustration. This is a waste of valuable energy.

Use the right tool for the job: Schedule your very best energy for that which is most difficult. Then, jump in and *do it*. Nine times out of ten, you will find this approach will break the dam and the rest will come pouring through on its own. For example, if you need to exercise, start by putting your workout clothes on in the morning or at noon when you are not exhausted by the day's work. If you feel you need to write a book or report, set aside your prime energy time and write the first paragraph. If you need to search for a job, plan to make at least one call first thing in the morning.

5. If you are having trouble determining ways to "act as if," start by eliminating each and every action which is contrary to your dream. Stop any habit or activity that in any way supports a reality different from the one you intend to create.

6. *Work is the ultimate acting as if.* That's why we are called "miracle *workers*." Work as hard as you can to make your dream real. Don't hold back here. Go for it—all the way.

Work is belief in motion. The demonstrator was a

very hard worker all his life. Look at how diligently he was working when the Miracle of the Loaves and Fishes occurred. He had already slaved away all day healing and teaching thousands of people before the manifestation occurred. He was obviously a very motivated and industrious person.

Follow his example and you will prosper. Dismiss any notion that you can get something for nothing. Miracles aren't magic. You have to come through with your end of the deal if you expect the universe to do its part. The only part that is magic is that when you do your share of the real work involved, the universe will return your effort ten times over. It's one of the best deals anywhere.

7. Establish the ninth condition in conjunction with the eighth condition: Be thankful that you can work. Bless your job, your employer, your coworkers, and all the fruits of your labor, and you will naturally rise to the top.

ENGAGING
THE CYCLE

ἔδωκε	τοῖς	μαθηταῖς	τοὺς	ἄρτους,
edoke	tois	mathitais	tous	artous,
He gave	to the	disciples	the	loaves,

οἱ	δὲ	μαθηταὶ	τοῖς	ὄχλοις,
oi	de	mathitai	tois	ochlois,
and	the	disciples	to the	crowds,

The Miracle of the Loaves and Fishes is characterized by a circular flow of energy and resources. A careful analysis of how the energy flows during the miracle easily reveals this.

As conditions one through nine are established, energy flows *toward* the demonstrator. Having established a condition of emptiness, things naturally move to him: The crowd follows him from the city. The boy in the crowd gives what little food he has to the disciples and the disciples pass it forward to Jesus. In the tenth step, the demonstrator causes the incoming flow to circle back so that it travels out and away from him: He returns the food to the disciples and the disciples give it back to the crowd. This sets up a circular current, a cycle. The manifestation process occurs *while* the energy is looping back. At the end of the miracle, when the remaining fragments are gathered and returned, the energy comes full circle—the circuit is complete, the engine primed for another powerful stroke.

Every enlightened person in history has tried to tell us that we receive as we give. It will always be true: What goes around comes around. The law of cause and effect that governs this process is quite precise. We reap just as we sow, and our return is always an accurate reflection of our release.

There is one important exception: When a circular current is established in conjunction with the other conditions of a miracle, resources can actually multiply *exponentially* as they pass around the circuit. Seeds that are sown by a miracle worker can grow many times over to produce an enormous harvest.

This phenomena is analogous to what happens as electricity flows through a transformer. As electrons flow around and around the series of circular coils within a transformer, the power is surprisingly increased. The voltage of the electricity that emerges from the transformer greatly exceeds the voltage of the electricity that enters. The same principle is at work in your own body. The biochemical reactions that sustain life are arranged in an intricate series of cycles referred to as metabolism. Like the coils of a transformer, these cycles are elegantly linked and connected. The wheels and gears of an intricate Swiss watch are crude by comparison.

What's fascinating is that the energy released as your biochemical cycles process the chemical bonds of the food you eat *far exceeds* that which is taken in. As you burn calories in the Krebs cycle and other biochemical loops within your cells, you produce heat and motion. The chemical energy that goes into your body and the energy that is generated balance exactly as predicted by the laws of thermodynamics. But traditional science fails to take into account that you also generate the brilliant light of consciousness. This increase is clearly "miraculous."

It is said that we are made in the image of God. This does not mean that we look like God: It means that our essence is the same as God's. Our life-sustaining systems are organized like the systems that sustain the very life of the universe, and operate in the same way. As above, so below. Just as a human being is an intermeshing system of dynamic cycles that generates consciousness, so is the universe.

This is very useful information for the aspiring miracle worker. Knowing that the energy of the universe flows through interlinked cyclical patterns will help you better align with the great flow. In order to fully synchronize with the energy currents of the world around you, it is important to shift from a linear mindset to a cyclical mindset. Failure to understand this has ruined many a life. As the ancient Greek philosopher Alcmaeon once observed, "Men perish because they cannot join the beginning with the end."

Activating the Tenth Condition

1. As energy begins to flow through your life, pass it on. Keep things moving. Receive the energy of others around you and release it quickly and efficiently. Your services will be in high demand. Constantly look for ways to send energy back around the circuit. When you receive, automatically look for a way to give something back. Work on this until it becomes a reflex.

If someone performs a favor or courtesy, look for ways to send the energy back without delay. Constantly turn the conversation back to the other person. When you are complimented or given credit, return the compliment. If it is inappropriate or impossible to return the energy to the sender, return it to someone else.

2. Be an excellent team player. The universe operates much like a championship basketball team. The ball is never still. It is passed around constantly. Winners never hog the ball.

3. Never drop the ball. Return your calls diligently. Answer your mail promptly. Pay your bills on time. When you are working with others, don't be the weak link in the chain. Be reliable, someone others can count on to react consistently and appropriately.

4. Remember that growth occurs in cycles. Consider the growth rings of a tree: even the greatest tree in the forest has weathered many droughts. Honor the ebb tide. Every wave has a trough. You can't be up all the time. When the tide goes out, don't panic—it will return. Never fight the current. Relax into the natural cycles of growth.

5. A smart captain uses an ebb tide to patch the holes in his vessel. Use any downtime constructively to prepare your vessel to receive efficiently when the flow returns.

The Eleventh Condition

RECEIVING

καὶ	ἔφαγον	πάντες,	καὶ	ἐχορτάσθησαν·
kai	efagon	pantes,	kai	echortasthisan.
and	ate	all,	and	were satisfied.

A beautiful story is told in the Second Book of Kings, in which the prophet Elisha is approached by a woman whose husband recently died. She is beside herself because she has been left with a great debt and has no way to repay it. As a result, the lender has notified her that he intends to take her two sons as slaves.

Elisha asks the woman if she has any assets at all. She tells him that she has a single jar of oil in the house—a valuable commodity. He then instructs the woman to go around to all her neighbors to collect empty jars, and makes a point of telling her to get as many of them as she can possibly find.

"Go into your house, shut the door, and pour the oil from your own vessel into the empty vessels you have collected," he tells her, "and when the empty vessel is full, set it aside." The widow follows his advice. She pours her jar of oil into the first empty vessel and when it is full, her sons give her another empty vessel. As the empty jars are filled, the oil keeps flowing and flowing. Finally, she asks her astonished boys to bring her another jar, but they tell her that none remains. All the vessels have been completely filled, and the woman now has enough wealth to pay her debt and live comfortably.

When no empty vessels remain, the story goes, the oil stops flowing. In other words, the supply is infinite; what we can *collect* from that infinite supply is limited only by the containers we prepare to receive the supply. Long ago, when I was poor, a wealthy mentor told me over and over with a booming laugh, "The secret to success is big pockets." So often we ask Spirit to provide but fail to prepare ourselves to collect the abundance that will appear.

Remember, *Spirit abhors a vacuum*. As soon as you prepare an empty container to receive, the universe will automatically begin mobilizing to fill it.

PAYING ATTENTION

We often think we are experts on receiving. "That's the easy part," we say. "Anyone can receive." But the fact is that we have much to learn in this area. Although receiving can be a simple, effortless matter, we complicate it in many unnecessary ways. When the mind is turbulent, confusion muddies the waters. Doubt and fear often keep us from recognizing and gracefully accepting the gifts of the universe. Life presents a bewildering array of complex opportunities and choices. Separating the wheat from the chaff can be tricky. It takes a clear and steady mind to discern which choices are gifts and which are painful illusions.

I have allowed doubt and confusion to keep me from gracefully receiving many times in my own life. For example, when I moved to the mountains years ago, I located nearly a dozen emergency rooms that offered employment. The first one that was offered, however, seemed unsuitable, and I rejected it. This, in spite of the fact that the recruiter in charge of this particular facility pressed me repeatedly to consider it.

Why did I reject that hospital? Actually, it had nothing to do with the hospital. I just didn't like the recruiter's manner on the phone. It was nothing more than that. She seemed a bit pushy and controlling in her efforts to place me. As a direct result, I settled on another ER and began working in it as soon as I moved.

The results were extremely painful. The opportunity I had chosen was far from optimal. I quickly found that working conditions at this facility were brutal. The hours were long and the duties involved were stressful beyond description. My coworkers were abrasive and difficult. After a year and a half of exhausting work, I was finally persuaded one day to cover a single shift at the first ER that had been offered. The regular doctor had fallen ill and the promise of double wages lured me grudgingly to accept. "Just this once," I grumbled.

Within a hour of arriving, I sheepishly realized that this was by far the best ER I had ever worked in. Working conditions here were infinitely superior. The doctors and nurses were friendly and easygoing. The equipment and backup were superb. Even the pay was better. Within a week, I signed a full-time contract and worked there happily for six years.

In retrospect I see I just wasn't paying attention. I wasn't able to receive, even though my abundance had been pressing in upon me from the start. The recruiter's "pushiness" was actually the universe trying to make itself clear. My irritation with her was nothing but my ego rearing its ugly head. If I had been truly perceptive, truly *receptive,* I could have saved myself several thousand hours of pain and stress.

LIVING THE DREAM

Accepting our abundance is only part of the process of receiving. We also have to know what to do with it when we get it. When it manifests, we have to allow it to thoroughly permeate our lives with joy, fun, and satisfaction. Carefully and consciously, we have to allow ourselves to be *filled*.

I recall what happened to a friend of mine who lived on a beautiful island in Puget Sound. This woman knew a great deal about visualization, affirmation, and faith. She had a great dream and worked diligently with her attitudes and projections to bring it about. She visualized living in the country with a man who loved her. She held true to her vision, and in time it manifested with startling accuracy. However, about a year later they grew apart and eventually separated. She had to move back into town. It appeared that her miracle had failed. "But why?" she wondered. "Why would the universe allow me to have my dream only to take it away?"

She consulted me. The problem was immediately obvious: She had been able to make her dream happen but unable to *live* the dream. Instead of letting it fill her, she gradually took it for granted. In time, the beautiful life she had created dissipated back into the realm of the unmanifest.

When a cherished dream manifests, the work is far from over. As the dream begins to appear, the real work is just beginning. Great care and vigilance must be exercised at this critical point to sustain the manifestation. This is done by letting the dream fill you completely. Gratitude plays a crucial role in this phase. You must open your eyes wide and pay constant attention to the wonder of your new circumstances. Let your miracle fill you with wonder, appreciation, and enthusiasm. Never take your blessings for granted. Fulfillment is an ongoing process that is never finished. Like attracts like and like sustains like. Positive states of consciousness brought your miracle to fruition and are the force which will *keep* it alive.

I once had a patient who fought a deadly cancer. Although his prognosis was very poor, he didn't allow this to deter his efforts. During his long months of surgery, chemotherapy, and radiation, he prayed fervently to be healed. He visualized. He said affirmations. He let go and released himself to the higher good. He did everything he possibly could, and against all odds he was miraculously cured.

After the danger had passed and his life had been restored, however, he went into a depression. He was so badly depressed, in fact, that he required therapy and medication to function. When the cancer was gone, I remember him asking me, "But now what am I supposed to do?" Now that he had his life back, he seemed to have no idea what to do with it. He moped around and couldn't seem to get his energy focused on anything productive. The effects were deadly. A year later, he relapsed and died within several months.

This man failed to be filled, failed to live the dream. He took his miracle for granted and his complacency killed him. Who knows how things might have been if he had allowed himself to receive, to let his new life fill him completely.

Activating the Eleventh Condition

1. Eat and be filled. Receive and let the energy and resources that flow into your life fill you with intense, joy, pleasure, fun, and gratitude. Work at this as though your life depended on it. It does.

2. Pay attention. Continue to quiet, clarify, and sharpen your mind with meditation. This will raise your consciousness and heighten your perception so that you will *recognize* your gifts when they come to you. As you know from your study of the other conditions, many of your most important gifts will take the form of seeds.

Your dream may not be delivered fully manifested on a silver platter. Don't miss the subtle leads which are the real gifts that can liberate you.

For example, the business section of your daily newspaper contains a vast amount of detailed knowledge about stocks. Hidden within this blizzard of symbols and numbers are a few pieces of crucial information that could easily make you independently wealthy within a few weeks. If you could *see* with perfect clarity, you could pick this information out and use it.

So it is with the everyday world which lies before you. Although you may not realize it, many important things you need to know to prosper and flourish are right in front of you. When you raise your consciousness with techniques like meditation, you will begin to *recognize* the information you need to make your dream become reality. Keep your eyes open. Look carefully through your mail. Listen to people. Pay attention to all the little things that "coincidentally" cross your path.

3. Be wide open in consciousness. The secret of success is big pockets—and lots of empty jars. But understand that for the most part, our pockets and jars are not physical in nature. Miracles operate primarily at the level of consciousness. Big pockets are formed by *thinking* big.

Cultivate a consciousness of unlimited potential. Believe that anything is possible. Avoid any limited, fearful thinking like the plague.

4. Understand the "lead-in" concept. Your big break may initially present itself as a trivial gift. Be gracious and accept even the little things that are offered to you in good faith. The universe may test you. Many times a tiny gift will lead to a much larger opportunity down the road. Follow the bread crumbs with care.

5. Develop a sense of worthiness. Never allow yourself to think you are not worthy. When you are centered in a compassionate mindset and are giving generously to the world around you, you are *automatically* worthy. You are a source of good and deserve to be supplied.

RECYCLING

καὶ	ἦραν	τὸ	περισσεῦον	τῶν	κλασμάτων,
kai	iran	to	perisseuon	ton	klasmaton,
and	they took	the	excess	of the	fragments,

δώδεκα	κοφίνους	πλήρεις.
dodeka	kopfinous	plireis.
twelve	handbaskets	full.

Once there was a man who had a terrible golf swing. No matter how hard he tried, he couldn't hit the ball straight and true. Month after month, year after year, he practiced. But his progress was marginal, and he continued to slice the ball on nearly every shot. He wasn't able to win a single game.

One day, a nationally known golf pro came to town and

the man scheduled a lesson with him. The pro took one look at his swing and immediately saw the problem: The man's swing had no follow-through. Once his club struck the ball, the man lost interest.

The golf pro worked with the man for about an hour, showing him how to complete his swing. The pro explained that what happens *after* the club strikes the ball is just as important as what happens before the club strikes the ball. With this simple advice, the man began to hit the ball with great power, and his once errant shots became straight and true.

The same principle should be applied to the conditions that bring about miracles. What happens after the manifestation has crystallized is just as important as what happens before. The flow of energy must never be abandoned once the dream becomes reality. When the desired results manifest, a certain follow-through must take place. Like a good golf swing, this follow-through will add considerable power to your actions and greatly increase the accuracy of your intent.

Following through also resets the mechanism so that everything is primed and ready for the next miracle. Finishing each cycle with an effective follow-through thus enables the miracle worker to continually gain momentum. Each miracle transpires more easily and more naturally than the last. A master eventually achieves enough momentum so that a realm is entered in which *everything* is effortlessly miraculous.

Careful translation of the original text sheds additional light on this subject. The Greek word that is traditionally translated as "excess" is *perisseuon*. According to *Strong's Exhaustive Concordance, perisseuon* can mean "excess," but can also refer to "a state of superabundance." What an interesting and very appropriate Greek word for Matthew to choose: When the conditions of a miracle are set into motion, the supply that manifests is so bountiful that it surpasses simple abundance and reaches a state of *super*abundance.

When this happens, there is *more* than enough for the miracle worker and everyone around him. However, even the excess should be carefully handled. The Alpha Passage indicates that any supply which goes unused should be gathered and not wasted. An extreme aversion to waste is one of the primary characteristics of the Infinite Intelligence. The universe is incredibly efficient, and evidence of this tendency can be observed everywhere. Nature recycles energy and resources with profound care at every level. Animals use oxygen and produce carbon dioxide as a byproduct. In a beautifully coordinated fashion, plants use this carbon dioxide as fuel and produce oxygen as a byproduct. Animals and plants recycle each other's waste products perfectly.

The same principle is at work elsewhere in our ecosystems. Plants use decayed material in the soil and water as food. Animals eat plants, grow larger, and eventually die. Their bodies are recycled through the process of decomposition and, once again, become food for plants. In our bodies, complex biochemical cycles use sugars, proteins, fats, and oxygen to produce energy. The end products of metabolic cycles are recycled and become fuel for the next cycle. Every possible calorie of energy is extracted with astonishing efficiency.

Anyone seeking to work miracles must honor this universal pattern. This is accomplished by carefully recycling energy and resources that pass through your life. If you do this, you will engage with the great cycles of the universe that can provide the energy for all the miracles of your life.

Activating the Twelfth Condition

1. Gather up the fragments: Don't throw *anything* away without asking yourself, "Is there some way this can be reused?" Recycle all of the physical resources that pass through your life.

Sort your cans and bottles and paper conscientiously. Compost all discarded organic matter. Be enthusiastic and supportive of all local and national recycling projects.

2. Cultivate the appropriate mindset when recycling. Each recycling effort is a sacred act that synchronizes you with divine purpose. Be clear and positive and reverent about this. Never allow yourself to feel that recycling is inconvenient or irritating. This is one indulgence you cannot afford.

3. Be reluctant to discard your possessions and tools as they age. Use everything to the maximum. Look for ways to repair and renew all your resources. Whenever possible, give your used possessions to charitable organizations that can sell or use them.

4. Close the loop. It's not enough to direct used resources to the proper channel. You also need to *buy* products made from recycled materials whenever possible. Make an effort to learn about such products. Make your voice heard: Ask your vendors to stock recycled products. Support the industries that produce them by buying them consistently.

5. Recycle your life. Be conscientious and responsible with your estate. Make sure you have a will. Be sure to include some key charitable ventures as beneficiaries.

Don't leave the follow-through of your life to others. Take conscientious steps now to see that your personal wealth and resources are channeled to the right places when you are gone.

6. Recycle your body. Whenever a blood drive comes around, do your part and give of yourself. Sign the section of your driver's license which authorizes organ donation and clear this with your relatives. Encourage your friends and relatives to do the same.

7. Recycle all of the mental and spiritual resources that pass through your life. Pass your knowledge on. Be a mentor, guardian, teacher, and benefactor. Share the *knowledge* of miracles you have gained within these pages and in your life.

Summary

THE BIG PICTURE

Years ago performers known as plate spinners would amaze and delight audiences. On stage they were surrounded by a number of vertical fiber glass poles much like stout fishing rods. A plate with a small rim on the bottom would be placed at the top end of a pole. Then the plate would be vigorously rotated. The plate would spin nicely at the top of the pole. After about twenty or thirty seconds the rotation of the pole would slow. The plate would then fall to the ground and break—unless the performer added more energy by manually rotating the pole once again.

The plate spinner would get seven or eight plates going at the same time. But he had to exercise great care to keep a close eye on each plate so that he could get it spinning again before rotation slowed and it crashed to the ground. A really good plate spinner was sometimes able to keep twelve plates spinning simultaneously.

Establishing the twelve conditions of a miracle is a bit like the spinning plate act: You have to get all of the conditions going at the same time in order to open the gate of heaven, the door into the dimension of the miraculous.

At first, this may seem virtually impossible. It is far from easy to get any twelve things going at the same time. The task may seem beyond your reach. In fact establishing and maintaining all twelve conditions simultaneously would be impossible if not for the fact that you have something going for you that a plate spinner does not. You have the ability to form *habits*. With positive habits, you can get some of the twelve plates to spin automatically. With practice, this will leave you free to pay attention to the three or four conditions that are most difficult for you.

A number of the twelve conditions are probably already habit for you. We all have certain spiritual strengths. You may already excel at compassion, meditation, giving, and recycling. With a few months of sincere effort you can get up to speed with another four of the conditions. This will allow you to concentrate fully on the four conditions that are most challenging.

Working all twelve conditions is not a magical trick. It is a way of *living*. Many positive effects can be experienced by living this way of life. Some of these benefits will be experienced right away, long before you become proficient at getting all of them to run at once. But the full effects will not be experienced until you have lived the way for a more extended time. Hopefully, you will spend the rest of your life honing your skills with the twelve conditions. As you do, you will become a miracle worker. You will come to see heaven.

A summary of the essential action steps for each of the twelve conditions is provided below. If you get discouraged or confused and don't know which step to concentrate on, review this list carefully. Think about your life and your attitudes. Which of these things have you allowed to deteriorate? Which action steps need your attention most?

THE FIRST CONDITION

Emptiness

- *Clarify* in your mind what you lack and what you need. Are you blocking your own flow by withholding this very thing from the world around you?
- Calmly *release* what you are withholding. Be *consistent and steady* in your release.
- *Expect* that the flow will reestablish itself. Form follows thought: Visualize the channels opening and reestablishing themselves within your life.

- Learn to meditate. Then *do* it. Practice consistently. Enjoy it.
- Spend time in nature; in quiet, solitary places.
- Walk and exercise your body every day.
- Consider occasional fasting.

THE SECOND CONDITION

Alignment

- With the eyes of Spirit, *see* the multitudes. Shift to a mindset of compassion, from concern over your own concerns to the concerns of others. At home and at work—in your microenvironment—be increasingly aware of others' problems and needs.
- When you learn of a problem or disaster, *do something* to help. Heal the sick. Become a lightworker: Heal with your mind and your heart.
- Fine-tune your synchronicity. Like small adjustments to the rigging of a sailboat, small, compassionate, and unselfish actions will help you move ahead in all your endeavors with tremendous speed.

THE THIRD CONDITION

Asking

- Formulate your request mentally. Work at this carefully until your request is clear.
- Dwell on the essence of the dream you seek to manifest. Know the *feelings* you really seek to experience.
- Put your request into words. Write your description of the essence on a piece of paper, place it in a prominent place, and read it frequently. This will help you keep your trajectory true to the mark.
- Keep things in general terms. Free the universe to use the widest variety of means to deliver the essence of the dream and quicken the manifestation process.
- Honor the principle of integral need. Make sure your needs are an integral part of your true evolution, an integral part of Spirit's true evolution. The universe will then have a vested interest in helping you.

THE FOURTH CONDITION

Maximizing

- Take an inventory of your existing tools and resources and blessings. Don't forget to include your talents, your health, your knowledge, and your other intangible resources.
- Whatever you focus on *expands*: Focus on what you have.
- Ask yourself: Are you maximizing what you already have? Take definitive steps to make absolutely sure that you are.

THE FIFTH CONDITION

Giving

- Become a regular, consistent giver.
- Above all else, seek to achieve a feeling of satisfaction and joy with your giving. Like attracts like. Your positive feelings will attract more similar feelings into *your* life.
- Be pure in your intent and remain anonymous when possible. Never attach any strings to a gift, however subtle.

- Expect your return to come from the universe—*never* from those to whom you give.
- Give consciously and carefully. Avoid automatic giving. *Think* about what you are doing and make a sincere effort to channel your gifts to the right places.
- Take care to remember your *microenvironment*. Charity begins at home.

THE SIXTH CONDITION

Grounding

- Stay grounded. Experience the present moment as much as possible.
- Become as a child. You will enter the garden by returning to your natural state of consciousness. Learn to play again. Make time to do things that are fun and try to spend some time with children, learning from them.
- Ground out physically. Take your shoes off. Wade in a stream. Walk on the lawn. Get outside and get in contact with mother earth.
- Work on your level of belief. Become as the woman in the crowd who touched the hem of the demonstrator's

robe: Know the power will flow to you, even if you barely touch the spirit in consciousness. If you can't make yourself believe, then fake it. *At all times, act and talk like you really do believe.*

THE SEVENTH CONDITION

Visualizing

- Remember the essence of your needs, the feelings you really want to end up experiencing. Don't see "things" manifesting. See yourself *having the feelings and experiences* that form the basis of your request.

- Using somatic visualization, *practice* experiencing the desired feelings in your entire body. This is an extremely powerful act. Work at this diligently and persistently. Like attracts like. The quality of your feelings will attract the appropriate circumstances that will support these feelings. Practice well.

- When you feel you are in heaven, you *are* in heaven.

- If you have a doubt, simply recognize it as a doubt and *turn it over to Infinite Intelligence to be quietly deactivated.* Once you become conscious of a doubt and turn it over to Spirit, it immediately ceases to generate effects within your reality, even though it may continue to run through your mind.

- Take care to incorporate the good of others in your visualizations.

THE EIGHTH CONDITION

Gratitude

- *Bless* your resources. All of them. All the time. Be acutely conscious of the gifts that have been entrusted to you. Cultivate a deep sense of appreciation.
- *Express* your feelings of gratitude in words. Make frequent positive comments about your health, your friends, your job, your house, your country, your life, and everything else you have been given.
- Don't *wait* for things to be grateful for. *Actively* search for things to be grateful for.
- While staying grounded in the moment, shift your mindset from one of jaded complacency and boredom to one of childlike wonder and amazement. The shift to wonderment is the door that opens into the higher dimension.
- *Speak well* of your dream, your life. *Never* speak any

negative words about anyone or anything. This can cause great damage. Strenuously resist the temptation to speak any words that support a reality different from the one you seek to create.

- When things are good, say good things. When things are bad, say *twice as many* good things.

THE NINTH CONDITION

Acting As If

- Stop dreaming and visualizing and start *doing.*
- Begin *now.* There is never any other time to begin.
- Avoid procrastination with all your might.
- Refuse to let any delay in the manifestation process surprise or discourage you. Expect a miracle, but expect it to unfold in its own time. Your dream will grow organically at its own rate.
- Accept your growth and stay relaxed. The more accepting you are about the time frame, the shorter it will be.
- Persist. No matter what happens, keep acting, keep going. Success has always belonged to the persistent.

Persistence can compensate for many other short-comings.

- Identify any snags, stumbling blocks, or difficult tasks that are holding you back.
- Break the necessary corrective action into several substeps and decide which is the very first action that must be taken.
- Next, determine a time of the week or time of the day when you are at your very highest energy. Carefully set that time aside for one purpose and one purpose only: to execute the first of the small steps that will break the stumbling block. *Schedule this time in writing and put it where you will see it frequently.*
- If you are having trouble determining ways to "act as if," start by eliminating each and every action that is contrary to your dream. Stop any habit or activity that in any way supports a reality different from the one you intend to create.
- *Work is the ultimate acting as if.* Work hard to make your dream real. When you do your share of the real work involved, the universe will return tens times the effort. Don't hold back here. Do everything you possibly can from your end to get things done.

THE TENTH CONDITION

Engaging the Cycle

- As energy begins to flow through your life, pass it on. Keep things moving. Receive the energy of others around you and pass it on quickly and efficiently.
- Constantly look for ways to send energy back around the circuit. When you receive, automatically look for a way to give something back.
- Be an excellent team player. Never *drop* the ball. Return your calls and answer your mail promptly. Pay your bills on time.
- Remember that growth occurs in cycles. Honor the ebb tide. Don't panic when the tide goes out. The flow always returns. Never fight the current. Relax into the natural cycles of growth. Use any downtime constructively, to prepare your vessel to receive when the flow returns.

THE ELEVENTH CONDITION

Receiving

- Eat and be filled. Receive and let the energy and resources that flow into your life fill you with intense joy, pleasure, and gratitude.
- Pay attention. Much of the information you need to prosper and flourish is right in front of you now. Continue to quiet, clarify, and sharpen your mind with meditation. Don't miss any subtle leads which could take you to the real gifts that will liberate you.
- The secret of success is big pockets. Be wide open in consciousness. Big pockets are formed by *thinking* big. Cultivate a consciousness of unlimited potential.
- Believe that anything is possible. Avoid any limited and fearful thinking.
- The universe may test you. Sometimes a tiny gift will lead to a much larger opportunity down the road. Follow the crumbs with care.
- Develop a sense of worthiness. You are a source of good and deserve to be supplied.

THE TWELFTH CONDITION

Recycling

- Gather up the fragments: Don't throw *anything* away without asking yourself, "Is there some way this can be reused?" *Recycle* all of the physical resources that pass through your life.
- Cultivate the appropriate mindset when recycling. Be clear and positive and reverent about this essential activity.
- Be reluctant to discard your possessions and tools as they age. Use everything to the maximum. Look for ways to repair and renew all your resources.
- Periodically, go through your closet and attic and storage rooms. Release things you no longer need or use to appropriate charities. An ebb tide offers a perfect time for this activity.
- Close the loop. Make an effort to *buy* products made from recycled materials whenever possible. *Ask* your vendors to stock recycled products.
- Recycle your life. Make sure you have a will. Be sure to include key charitable ventures as beneficiaries.

- Recycle your body. Participate in blood drives and make arrangements for organ donation.
- Recycle all of the mental and spiritual resources that pass through your life. Pass your knowledge on. Be a mentor, guardian, teacher, and benefactor.

Acknowledgments

I would like to thank the following individuals for their tremendously positive influences on my life and this book:

Nancy and Paul Franzenburg, for being such amazing and exceptional parents. Judy Boller, for outstanding emotional intelligence and intuitive input during the critical time this book was made known to the public.

Michael Metzler, M.D./Ph.D., Robin and Quent Johnson, Mickey and Sean Houlihan at Wind Over the Earth studios, Kit Hersey, Jimmy Twyman, Pril Snyder, Les Kahn, Summer Jones, Wind Hughes, Melinda Ryles, Shelley Smith, Colleen Williams, Marilyn Castilaw, Hon. Carol Glowinsky, Bigi Schanz, Margaret Lembo, Jon and Matt, Dr. Mark Albert, Dawn Rasmussen, Ben Fuchs, and the Elliotts and Barlows, for being my best friends.

Larry and Donna Lee Dennis, for discovering the book one Saturday morning, and Rev. Dr. Mary Manin Morrissey at the Living Enrichment Center, for subsequently bringing the book to the attention of thousands. My dear friends at the Boulder Campus Group, Brad Sykes, Chandler, Nicky, Rosia, Rich, and David, for their awesome spiritual support and guidance. Rev. Sharon Connors at Unity Village, Rev. Jeanette Freeman, Rev. Scott Awbrey, and Dr. Michael Mirdad for support and friendship above and beyond the call of duty.

Lora Barlow, for years of friendship and amazing intellectual and spiritual discourse surrounding the book. The Jeff Herman Literary Agency, for believing, Lori Rosen, for consultation on the concept and initial drafts, Colleen Cary, for inspired work on the initial manuscript, Isadoras Doxas, Ph.D., for initial Greek proofing, and Marilyn Cohen, for a beautiful design of the first two editions, and Timothy Meyer, for his meticulous revisions of the Greek in this edition.

Finally, I would like to thank all the ministers and congregants around the country who have formed Twelve Conditions study groups and, in particular, the seventy groups in the Denver metropolitan area. The book wouldn't be where it is today without your diligence and faith.

ABOUT THE AUTHOR

Todd Michael, D.O., FACOFP, is a writer, speaker, workshop presenter, and board-certified family practitioner. He was the medical director of a level III emergency room and trauma center while writing his first book, *The Evolution Angel*. He currently practices integrative, anti-aging, and fitness medicine at Clinix Life Enhancement Center in Centennial, Colorado. He has a special interest in natural hormone balancing. Dr. Michael's undergraduate degree is in psychology, from Iowa State University, and he was accepted into the Mensa Society in 1985. He is an accomplished artist and musician working from Essene Studios and lives with his son, Julian, in Boulder, Colorado.

His pastimes include distance rollerblading, snowboarding, mountain biking and mountaineering, and exploring the landscapes and hot springs of Colorado. He works with a number of charities including Children International, Amnesty International, and a variety of environmental causes.

TO LEARN MORE

Your comments, stories, and questions are always most welcome. Please visit us at *www.TwelveConditions.com* for information on Dr. Michael's other books, audio and video products, and speaking engagements. To schedule a personal phone appointment for life coaching or a workshop for your organization, call 303-527-3144.